Edward Everett Hale

The Fortunes of Rachel

Edward Everett Hale

The Fortunes of Rachel

ISBN/EAN: 9783337266981

Printed in Europe, USA, Canada, Australia, Japan

Cover: Foto ©ninafisch / pixelio.de

More available books at **www.hansebooks.com**

The Fortunes of Rachel

BY

EDWARD EVERETT HALE

AUTHOR OF "THE MAN WITHOUT A COUNTRY," "HIS LEVEL BEST," "HOW TO DO IT," "IN HIS NAME," "TEN TIMES ONE IS TEN," "CHRISTMAS IN A PALACE," ETC., ETC.

"To be thrown upon one's own resources is to be cast in the very lap of Fortune; for our faculties then undergo a development and display an energy of which they were previously unsusceptible."—B. FRANKLIN.

NEW YORK
FUNK & WAGNALLS, PUBLISHERS
10 AND 12 DEY STREET
1884

CONTENTS.

CHAPTER I.
The Baikal 5

CHAPTER II.
Land Ho! 12

CHAPTER III.
A New World 20

CHAPTER IV.
Hitchin 31

CHAPTER V.
The Demands of Society 39

CHAPTER VI.
Gayety and Charity 51

CHAPTER VII.
Another New World 61

CHAPTER VIII.
Is it Possible? 82

CHAPTER IX.
Forgotten Treasure 90

CHAPTER X.
Lake Constance 98

CONTENTS.

CHAPTER XI.
PARTING 114

CHAPTER XII.
THOMAS'S CONCERT 120

CHAPTER XIII.
THE ANCILLARY ESTABLISHMENT 125

CHAPTER XIV.
HUDDLESTON'S 187

CHAPTER XV.
CHICAGO REVISITED 145

CHAPTER XVI.
THE CRY IS STILL THEY COME 154

CHAPTER XVII.
CLOUD AND STORM 166

CHAPTER XVIII.
CRISIS 176

CHAPTER XIX.
BACK AGAIN 187

CHAPTER XX.
RACHEL'S ANSWER 196

CHAPTER XXI.
NEW YEAR'S DAY INDEED 203

CHAPTER XXII.
OLD FRIENDS AND NEW 212

CHAPTER I.

THE BAIKAL.

> " The direful spectacle of the wreck,
> I have with such provision in mine art
> So safely ordered, that there is no soul—
> No, not so much perdition as a hair
> Betid to any creature in the vessel."
>
> *The Tempest.*

"Have we really walked an hour?"

Rachel said this with unaffected surprise, as she heard the ship's bell tang-tang, tang-tang. It was four bells— six o'clock in the afternoon.

"I am sorry to say it is really an hour," said John Wolff. "But certainly a very short hour. May I join you when you take your walk to-morrow?"

But Rachel either did not hear or did not care to answer. She joined her father and mother, who had been taking a walk much less formidable, and then, bidding Mr. Wolff good-by, went down-stairs, as she always did, with her mother to see that she had her cocoa as she liked it, and was put comfortably to bed.

Rachel and her father and her mother belonged to that utterly undefined and undefinable race on a passenger ship called second-class passengers. They are not by any means steerage passengers. They are not by any means first-class passengers. But there can be little doubt that they are cabin passengers. Precisely what are their rights on deck he would be a very wise man who should say. This is certain—for Rachel is the living evidence of it—that, when the doctor is good-natured and the captain chooses to have it so, a nice girl like Rachel can take her constitutional on deck while the first-class passengers are in the saloon at dinner, and that nobody will think or say that the world is coming to an end. So it was that it happened, that on this particular Thursday afternoon Rachel and John Wolff had been taking their constitutional together. John Wolff was in no sort a second-cabin passenger. He had an inner stateroom, that is true. But he ranked, in the hierarchy of the ship, with the people who paid the most. He had a knack, however, of finding out the people he wanted to know, whether they were parted from him by wainscots or by étiquettes. In this case he and Rachel Finley's father had met forward one day, and Wolff had asked Mr. Finley for a light. They had come to be well acquainted, first, because they both were interested in some Irish children who were playing jack-straws; second, because they both had dabbled in photography; third, because they were both stanch Republicans; Wolff, with the handy experience of republican government, which comes of course to an American; Finley, because he had been the principal manager in a radical club in his home in the North of England. Thus was it that one afternoon Finley had introduced John Wolff to his wife, and that the young man had, the next day, taken the hour's walk with Rachel which she would else have taken with her father. Rachel was no longer a little girl. She was fully fourteen, and was tall for her age.

Yes, Mrs. Finley was, on the whole, going through the misery of the voyage better than any one had hoped —better than she had hoped. Wretchedness it was all —that was of course. Still, she could drag herself up-stairs in the latter part of the day. She had to-day even made the wretched attempt at a little walk. She was quite proud, and Rachel was quite proud, when, after the cocoa and the toast, the girl had undressed her mother, had put her to bed and kissed her, and tucked her up comfortably. She promised she would sleep, and sleep in fact she did.

And so did Rachel sleep, more comfortably than she had yet done any night, because her mother was so quiet. She waked once or twice, but it was only to count the engine throbs two or three times, and she was dreaming, really dreaming, of the brook at Sandford, when—

"CRASH!"

And there was no dreaming more. The whole berth trembled under her. A sort of heavy pulse seemed to beat in everything, below and above. Then the engine-throb again, and cries above. Rachel waited on her elbow. She heard her father run along the little passage to the bigger passage. She could not make out one word from the talk, not loud but earnest, which followed. Then he came back.

"Dress yourself as quick as you can, Rachel; but do not hurry. We have struck something, or something has struck us. You may as well be on deck, and I will bring your mother to you."

"Let me help my mother dress."

"No, dear child, no. She is used to me as well as you. And, as I tell you, there is plenty of time. Perhaps there is no need for alarm at all."

So such things always begin. Nor did Mr. Finley lie to her or to himself when he said all this. But, all the same, when Rachel's mother joined her on the upper deck after ten minutes, she knew, Rachel knew, and they all knew, that the ship was going down. The little

French fishing steamer which had run into them was burning blue lights some two hundred yards away, and even Rachel's inexperienced eye could see that her head was sunk much below her stern. In truth, her forward compartment was already full. On board the Baikal they knew by this time that their own condition was scarcely better. But everything was orderly. Groups were forming, as the officers of different boats were telling off their respective parties, and giving, not in very loud tones, their instructions. Some of the people had not imagination enough to be excited. Some had too much to be afraid. There was strangely little sobbing, questioning, or crying. It almost seemed as if people were shipwrecked every day.

"Thank God, we are together!" said Rachel's mother to her as the girl sat on the deck and held her hand. "How glad I am that your father did not come without us!"

"Glad indeed, dear mother; nothing seems wrong now that I have you and him." And at the moment her father joined them. He had been working with the ship's surgeon among those very Irish emigrants with whom his kindness had made him a sort of master, and who were fully willing to accept his authority.

"It is certain we must all take the boats," he said in a low tone to the others. "The fisherman is worse hurt than we are. He cannot help us, and we cannot help him. This vessel is steadily settling. In ten minutes there will be no fires in the engine-rooms, and after that it is all a question of time. But the mate yonder says it is well for us that there is so little sea, only they all wish it were lighter—I mean that there were no fog."

And then Rachel observed for the first time that once a minute a cannon was fired from the deck forward.

She had heard the sound before, but it had not occurred to her that this was "the minute-gun at sea." Heavens! How often she had laughed behind her Aunt Ann's back when the old lady had sung "The minute-gun at sea," and had pounded fourteen white ivory bass keys to give vigor to the explosion. And these were real minute-guns!

Steady discipline told. And it was well for them now that they had so few passengers. The Baikal was not a regular packet. She was on an extra trip, and in each grade of passage the passengers were only those who, by one accident or another, were left over from fuller vessels. The officers therefore did not lie, as during these hours of slow sinking they steadily told all the landsmen that there was room enough in the boats for each and all. Indeed, it was well for the *morale* of everybody that they were told off, as they were, into these little parties. They began to know each other and to know their chiefs. Rachel, in her ready, healthy way, soon made friends with the two red-faced children of the Irishwoman who, at first howling with horror, was now well content with the prospect before her. The stewards who belonged to their boat were fairly joking as they contended with other stewards, which should have a certain box of Boston crackers, and which a certain tub of butter for boat stores. The women sat and saw such provisions for housekeeping going on with new confidence in this boat voyaging. Surely, things could not be very hard for them if the men could laugh or even quarrel about bread and butter. But the women could see that the Baikal's deck was nearer to the water-line. On the main deck it was clear to anybody that her hours, perhaps her minutes, were all counted. And so at last the order came cheerily and civilly, as if it were an every-day affair. One of the warrant officers ordered the stewards out from the quarter-boat, which still hung upon the davits, and said, "Now, ladies, we are ready for you. John, give Mrs. Finley your hand. Watch your chance, Biddy. I'll hand you the babies," and, one by one, his six women were placed in their seats in the boat. A seaman before and one aft tended the ropes which were to lower her to the water. The other men would not enter her till she was afloat.

Rachel was the last to enter. Confident in her own steady step, she carried with her her mother's well-packed bag, almost as heavily laden as the good Elizabeth's bag in the "Swiss Family Robinson." She reached the boat, stepped on one gunwale as she gave the bag into her mother's arms, and at that instant the Baikal gave the first lurch she had given that morning. The girl tripped, started, and fell a dozen feet into the sea.

She rose like a cork. All those visits to Aunt Ann at Bishop's Wearmouth were not in vain. In a minute she was fresh on the water surface and called out "All right!" In a minute more the first officer, who in his own boat was lying just outside, had shot in to the Baikal; a young man forward had reached over and caught Rachel at the elbow. A minute more and he dragged her in.

"She is all right. She is all right. We will keep her till you come down."

Then they pulled back to their station of observation. And now the embarkation went forward rapidly. At each side of the great ship one regular gangway enabled a steady procession to move down and go on board with a certain system. Two of the larger boats took in their cargoes thus. The others were laden above, so far as their women folk went, and were lowered when they were ready. Poor Rachel was the only passenger who took the flying passage, unless the butcher's dog, who was ignominiously kicked overboard, is to be counted as a passenger.

Rachel sat, not shivering, watching the whole scene. She was wrapped in a heavy ulster coat which Mr. Wolff had in the boat with him. It was Mr. Wolff who had leaned over the gunwale and had hauled her in.

The poor Baikal! She was lower and lower. That young Cambridge lad who had been steadily firing his minute-guns was called in, and that voice was silent. He ran down the few steps yet above the water, and sprang into the doctor's boat. Poor Captain Ryland stood alone at the open gangway.

"Mr. Winter."

"Ay, ay, sir!" and the boat shot up to the step.

The poor captain stepped in. "There is not a cockroach on board, unless he wants to stay."

"They have all had their chance. Give way, men."

"Give way," repeated the coxswain.

And the boat sprung off from the unfortunate Baikal. The little fleet lay for half an hour—or was it so long,—all on board watching the gray form which still loomed through the darkness of the fog, when, with a sudden lurch, the smoke-stacks pitched forward, and in five seconds the whole was gone.

"Mr. Winter," cried the captain, "you understand your orders. Keep me in sight. No one is to make any haste. The course is west-south-west one half west."

"Ay, ay, sir!"

And Mr. Winter passed the direction to the boats next to him. The little flotilla was to work slowly along in the expectation, well-nigh a certainty, that before night some passing vessel on the great highway between two continents would see them and save them.

CHAPTER II.

LAND HO!

"Not alms, but a friend."

But the fog was too heavy.

Night fell, and there was no rescue. And all day long nobody had said a word about transferring poor Rachel to the boat in which were her father and her mother.

Alas! they had other things to think of than one which would break the line of voyage of the little squadron.

Night fell. Till night they had succeeded in keeping together. And after nightfall an occasional "Halloo!" would bring an answer from one boat or another. To Rachel the whole day had been putting her strangely at ease. Had she lived in this boat for months? The men petted her—their only woman passenger—and with all their rough attentions made her at ease. No sail had been set, and so the little bit of canvas which the boat had, had been passed aft and folded for a sort of long cushion, which she might stretch herself upon quite at length. Mr. Wolff's ulster and Mr. Atwood's heavy pea-jacket were both hers. Her own ill-fated wraps had been held up on the boat-hooks and oars to dry, as far as anything would dry in that dismal fog. She had wrung out her stockings and had rubbed her feet warm. There had been a thousand curious things to watch and to ask about, and so, at night, boat life seemed to Rachel as a thing almost as much of course as cabin life had seemed the night before.

"Only we did not get our walk before sunset, Mr. Wolff," she said.

She fell asleep. And she slept soundly. Indeed, it was after one o'clock when the coxswain, who at the helm was next her, touched her and woke her. The girl started. "Please, miss, listen, and tell what you hear."

"Hear—nothing but the waves. Oh, yes, there it is. Why, it is a horn—the long wail of a horn."

"Yes, miss, that is a fog-horn. Now, where away is it, miss?"

The girl pointed without hesitation. "It is there."

"Thank you, miss. I thought so, miss. But two is surer than one, miss." Then to his sleeping crew:

"Halloo! Attention! Let fall! One, two, give way!"

And the word passed immediately that a fog-horn had been heard. Then there was great search for a bugle. But it was not to be found. Somebody had had it, but nobody had seen it. After fifty strokes the coxswain stopped his men, hushed them all, listened again, and again all hands agreed as to the direction of that most mournful yet most hopeful wail.

"Now, all together, lads, cheer!" And one long "Halloo-o-o!" rang out in unison.

"Please, miss, will you hail him? They do say a woman's voice goes farther."

And Rachel, with her very best, as you need not doubt, rang out her woman's "Halloo!" good ten notes higher than the coxswain's.

Fifteen minutes more, and there was no doubt.

"Come round under our lee. A woman, you say?

Boys, make fast your ladder to the rail. Send her up first. Now you're all safe, marm. Any other women folks? Where be ye all from? Any more on you?"

It was the Gloucester fishing-boat William Wallace which had picked up the lost voyagers.

"Guess it was you we heerd," said the eager skipper when the boat was secured. "They say a woman's voice carries farthest when it's kind o' foggy."

And then began counsel and effort, back and forth, firing of muskets, blowing the horn, anything which might call the other boats from their hiding-places. But in two days' time the skipper found no other boat. There was clearly no good in staying where they were, and, as his fare was made, he bore away for Boston Bay.

"Never you fear for the others," said he a thousand times to Rachel. "The Calabria has them all. I spoke her jest as the sun went down, or jest when he would ha' gone down had there been any sun. Never you fear."

And after nine days the William Wallace came to an anchor half a mile off Long Wharf in Boston.

"May as well run into Boston, seein' the wind's at the east. Jest as well for these here passengers. They can see their folks easier, and I can go over and have a talk with Cap'n Babson." So they did not run into Gloucester Bay but into Boston Harbor.

"Now we shall hear where your folks be, Miss Rachel," said the skipper cheerfully, as at nine in the morning he bade Rachel good-by and rowed on shore.

But he did not find "where her folks was." He reported to the *Advertiser* ship-news officer, as his wont was, to be told at once that he had brought the first news of the Baikal's loss. All the good fellow's hopes were blasted in the moment. That he should telegraph to

New York or cable to Liverpool for her father, that he should go back to her and tell her all was well, he had been quite sure. Now he must make some better provision for her than the stateroom on the William Wallace, which by courtesy was called the captain's cabin. And he must make this provision " right away."

"What in the world do they do with gals that is picked up afloat at sea?"

The friendly reporter did not know. But he did know the way to what is called "the Chardon Street Bureau," and thither the captain went, only stopping to telegraph to his partner at Gloucester of his return, of the fare taken, and of the seamen and others rescued.

At the Bureau he passed through a hall where were loitering half a dozen sad-looking Irishmen, and one or two older men in tattered clothes, bent a good deal in the back and legs. More to the inquiry in his eyes than to any word of his, they answered by pointing him in to a busy office at the left, where he told his story.

The quiet gentleman on duty replied, "Eight seamen, you say, four emigrants, and a girl. Very well; if anybody needs anything, let them come here first. They have no clothes?"

"Oh, most of the men have their kits. I do not think the sailors will trouble you. It's the gal. She's nothin' but the clothes she is in—and we don't know where her father and mother be. They's in another boat, you see, and like as not they's gone back to Liverpool. She's a nice gal, say fourteen years old."

"And where is she?" said the patient officer.

"I tell you she's in my cabin now. I would not land her till I knew where to bring her."

"Oh, bring her here, of course, if she has no friends. We shall see to her." And he rang his bell. "Ask

Miss Child to have the goodness to come to me.—Miss Child, I think this is your case rather than ours. The captain here has picked up an English girl at sea. She is on board his boat. Captain, when will you have her here?"

"Wall, we'll both be here at half-past eleven, or say we'll call it eleven. I'll go aboard now and bring her right away."

"You say picked up at sea! Has she any clothes?" said the sympathizing lady.

"She has what she swum in, that's all," replied the captain, on a broad grin.

"And how big is she?" persisted Miss Child.

"Big? Wall, she's a good-sized gal of fourteen, as tall as that Irish gal in the entry; a nice gal, with nice ways, and the things she has is good," added the captain eagerly, by way of recommendation of his favorite.

"I will send up to the Provident, and her clothes shall be ready before you come," said Miss Child. "Here is my card. Bring her direct to me, at Number 93."

From office to office through the Charity Bureau ran the romantic news that a girl was to be brought in at eleven o'clock who had been picked up swimming in the Atlantic Ocean nine days from land. Each office was on its mettle to supply what the proprieties and fashions of Boston might find necessary for such a waif. And so, when poor dazed and astonished Rachel appeared with the captain at Number 93, there was provision enough there in every detail of equipage for twenty mermaids, had they been so fortunate as to take passage on the William Wallace. What was more to the point, perhaps, certainly what was most to poor Rachel's needs here, were two sympathetic, eager women, only anxious to strip her and to clothe her anew from head to toe, and a good deal disappointed indeed to see how nicely the girl had arrayed herself, and that, after nine days, her clothes were dry. For a box of new boots was lying open, from which her feet were to be fitted; piles of underclothing were to be tried; stockings, frocks, sacks, and even bonnets had been brought into the little room which had been seized for a dressing-room. There was no nonsense in this exuberant sympathy, but there was no lack of the sympathy; and to the admiring captain Rachel appeared in half an hour with no sign left upon her of her sudden plunge.

"You need give yourself no anxiety, captain," Miss Child was saying. "If it is necessary, I shall take her home with me to-night. But it is not necessary. You seem to forget that this is what we are for."

"For? How often do you have gals fished out of the sea on the Banks?"

Miss Child laughed. "Not often. But into these offices every year come ten thousand people not as well off as our little friend is, and just as ignorant what is to happen to them. We are here because they come, and so, as I say, we are not unused to taking care of them. But, my dear child," she said to Rachel, "I do not often see as nice a girl as you." And then the genuine New England shyness settling down on her after so long an address, she said, with the first instinct of true hospitality in all lands, "Are you not hungry? Miss Smith, I cannot well leave. Will you take her round to Mrs. McGill and ask her to give you both some chowder? Captain, go in with them. We cannot quite match your Cape Ann chowder, but we will keep you from starving."

And Miss Smith led the way laughing to the Temporary Home next door. Again the miraculous story was told that this girl had been picked up swimming in the middle of the Atlantic. Matters were well advanced, before the captain discovered this misapprehension and gave a more correct statement. But, as usually happens, the marvellous story held its place and the more stupid fact was forgotten. Mrs. McGill eagerly produced soup-plates and spoons and crackers and salt, and at a table covered with glazed cloth they sat at their lunch. It was much such a meal as Rachel had joined in at noon every day on board the William Wallace. It was neatly served. It was something the girl had never eaten in Yorkshire. But, all the same, she liked it. She was young. She was hungry. The chowder was hot and savory and nourishing. What if the spoons were pewter and the stout earthen plates knocked and cracked at the edges?

When they came back, Miss Child again assured the good skipper that he need not wait. "We will see she is well off, and Mr. Canfield says she shall have the very first news of her father. Leave us your address and you shall hear too." So the skipper left the address of his Gloucester firm. "But, my dear Rachel, if I'd had any home now, you know you would have gone back with me." And his eyes filled to overflowing as he made this first reference to the old home that was not. And poor Rachel—little wonder—jumped into his arms and kissed him.

When he was gone the poor child felt, as well she might, that she was indeed alone.

The good friend who had seen to her outfit did not misapprehend the position. She said a word or two of good cheer to poor Rachel, but rightly guessed that the true comfort was to be found in occupying her with new sights and sounds.

"And so, my dear girl, Rachel—is that your name?—while we are waiting for news from New York, Miss Smith here shall take you to walk, to see the wonders of this wild America. See if you cannot bring me home a little lion cub from the Common.

"Miss Smith, run up-stairs and put on your things. Tell them in the office that I say you are needed on important duty in the Fifth Ward. Come down here and take our little Rachel up to the Common. Show her the sights, and be back here at two."

And then, in a half aside, half confidential to Miss Smith, she said, "I'll have some one here to meet her then."

CHAPTER III.

A NEW WORLD.

"The broad-armed trees above it growing,
The clear breeze through the foliage blowing."

So Rachel and Miss Smith worked their way through Cambridge Street, which is the crowded central ganglion of the circulation of Boston, where men, women, horses, cars, carts, and carriages from the north meet and pass boys, girls, dogs, cats, express wagons, and loads of moving furniture from the south. They passed Scollay Square, and Miss Smith pointed out the statue of Winthrop to Rachel, and explained to her how the first people came over. They worked their way along to the Common, and the poor sea-tossed girl was regaled with the sight of green grass and overhanging trees. Miss Smith led her to the Frog Pond, in the hope that the fountain might be playing, never so shyly. But alas! water was scarce that summer, and there was no such display.

But there was what was better—an army of boys, not to say girls, sailing their tiny boats upon the tiny "lake." And Rachel exulted in the steadiness of the earth beneath her, in the fragrance of new-cut grass. She sympathized with the feeling of an expert in every shipwreck, and found herself giving counsel how a sail made from a writing-book should be fastened that it might best woo the south wind.

Of a sudden a surprised voice :

"Why, my dear Miss Rachel, is this you ?"

The girl turned in wonder that any one should know her, and in hope, in all this unknown continent. The speaker was Mr. Wolff, whom she had not seen since they parted at breakfast on the fishing-boat. She had had no chance even to bid him good-by.

"Why, Mr. Wolff!" she said. "I am so glad to see you. It seemed so rude that I left you without even saying good-by, when I wanted to thank you so much, and the captain, and all for your kindness to me."

"The captain and all were sure of that," replied he, pleasantly. And he took a seat by her, and made her sit down again. He bowed to Miss Smith and went on :

"All of us went ashore, just to report ourselves, and thought we should find you on board when we came back with news. But when we came back our little bird had fled."

"And you know there is no news," said the girl, with her eyes filling.

"No, none yet. How should there be ? There can be no news till they get to Liverpool, and that cannot be till to-morrow or next day."

Thus spoke Mr. Wolff, with that steady desire to comfort a woman which holds so important a place in the conversation of kind-hearted men. He forgot, or pretended to forget, what Rachel did not for a moment forget, that only a moment before he had said they went ashore for news and expected it.

"And now, Miss Rachel, where are you, and what can we do for you ? The captain goes to New York to-day. And I know he will take you with him if you will. For me, I am going to Chicago to-night, on my way to my friends, who live three hundred miles beyond.

I will gladly take you to my mother, who will take, oh, beautiful care of you till we hear from your father."

But Rachel was quick enough to discern, even in the tone of his voice, his own feeling that this would not be a wise thing to do. Still she was grateful for the offer. And Mr. Wolff was the only connecting link which she had with her father. She answered, slowly:

"Three hundred miles! That would be a great way to go while we are waiting. How far is the other place? How far is Chicago?"

"Oh, my dear girl," Miss Smith broke in here, "that is all out of the question. Chicago is a day and a half away; it is more than a thousand miles. The gentleman is very kind. But you will stay with us till we hear from your father."

Mr. Wolff bowed. Who "us" might be he did not know. But he could see that Miss Smith understood herself, and was a lady.

"Can I be of any service? Can I write or telegraph? Or can I not lend Miss Rachel some money? I have already drawn on my father by telegraph, and I am rich indeed."

But Miss Smith was decided. Rachel needed neither travelling companions nor loans of money, certainly not from gentlemen whose names even Miss Smith did not know. She thanked Mr. Wolff not austerely, said "we" should be quite able to care for Miss Finley, and changed the subject squarely from the future to the past by asking some question about the shipwreck.

Mr. Wolff yielded to her evident will. But he yielded in wonder. He knew perfectly that, four hours before, Rachel Finley was an utter stranger on the edge of an unknown continent. Columbus was not less known to the Inca of Peru on the morning of the 21st of October,

1492. And now here was Rachel Finley, on terms of alliance, offensive and defensive, with a ladylike woman whose name he did not know, but who spoke of "we" and of "us" as one having authority.

But Mr. Wolff thought, perhaps thought rightly, that he had exhausted the privileges of a fellow-traveller in the suggestions he had already made. Possibly a young man of twenty was not the best conceivable guide, counsellor, and friend for a penniless girl of fourteen flung ashore by the sea.

He let the talk take the drift it would. And when Miss Smith determined that they had stayed long enough he gave them his escort back to the "Bureau." Here, of course, the mere official aspect of the place answered some of his questions, though they did not wholly satisfy him. At Miss Child's door he was significantly enough advised that his presence was not needed further. And after some inquiries in the other offices he went his way.

Meanwhile Miss Child had been as good as her word. So soon as the two had left her to "see the sights," Miss Child had walked through to the telephone in Mr. Patten's room.

"Give me the Adams House."

And they gave her the Adams House.

"Is Mrs. Lois Winchell in?"

The Adams House waited, and in a minute Mrs. Lois Winchell announced herself as waiting for news.

"I am Miss Child, of the Employers' Aid. I think we have what you want. She is an English girl, neat and nice; has just been rescued from a wreck. She has now no father and no mother, but they may turn up at any minute."

And Mrs. Lois Winchell answered,

"Can she read and write?"

Poor, disgraced Miss Child, in the excitement of the morning, had neglected to ask. But she replied,

"I think so. I am almost sure. You will like her when you see her."

"What religion is she?" persisted Mrs. Lois Winchell.

Again Miss Child was at a loss. But unflinchingly she replied, "Oh, that is all right. You had better come and see her."

"What shall I do when her father comes?"

"Send to me for another," said the unblushing Miss Child, who knew perfectly how large were her resources.

"I had not meant to go out," said Mrs. Winchell, doubtfully. But the woman who hesitates is lost.

"Then I must let her go somewhere else," said Miss Child boldly.

"Oh, well. If you cannot wait, I will come. Only my sister is spending the day with me. I will be at your office at two."

"She shall be here at two. Good-by."

"Good-by." And Miss Child returned to her office and sent three spinners from Lancashire to Holyoke, four maids of all work from Ireland to Coos County, five telegraph operators to Nova Scotia, and six chambermaids to the Mermaid Hotel at Nantasket. As the last of the Mermaids retired Miss Smith returned with Rachel, and in five minutes more Mrs. Lois Winchell, on the stroke of two o'clock, came in.

"Dear Miss Child, where should I be without you? You are as good as your word. When I left Hitchin this morning, as I sat in the depot, Mary Fifield was there. And she said, 'Mrs. Winchell, if you stay in Boston till you get a girl you will be there a week.' 'Well,' said I, 'there are worse places to be in. I shall see the Vokeses every night. And next Sunday I shall hear Mr. Clarke preach, and to-day I shall send for Susan to come and spend the day.' But all the time I said to myself, 'The Lord will provide. And if Miss Child has not the right girl for me I am very much mistaken.'"

All this address Mrs. Winchell made despite of signals from poor Miss Child that it would be better were she silent. Silence was not Mrs. Winchell's forte.

"Shipwrecked, you say? Was she on the Nautilus? That was dreadful. The Baikal? No, I had not heard of the Baikal. Oh, she is here? What, this nice little girl? Oh, I did not understand you. And does she want to come to me?"

Then Miss Child took the floor, and with authority to which she was quite used, and which was quite necessary in her position, she suppressed Mrs. Lois Winchell for some minutes. She explained what the reader knows—that Rachel was temporarily a waif, was without any father or any mother. But she took the most confident view as to the present existence on this earth, or the sea which belongs to it, of both the father and the mother. Still, if they were taken back to Liverpool, as seemed wellnigh certain, Rachel Finley would be in America wellnigh a month before they could join her. While that month passed she must be somewhere. Where better, that somewhere, than in Mrs. Lois Winchell's home at Hitchin? This was the triumphal question with which Miss Child closed her address.

She had put her points well, and Mrs. Winchell anticipated and accepted her conclusion.

Indeed, she accepted it before it was made. She had long since learned that, on such points, Miss Child's judgments were more reliable than her own.

But Miss Child did not expect, did not indeed permit, that she should answer. "Rachel, dear, go into my room with Mrs. Winchell and talk with her by yourselves."

And as the girl went in, Miss Child, who knew in her own heart how closely she was drawn herself to the poor little thing, whispered to her, "Do nothing but what you like. You are with friends here. But she is a friend too. Do not be afraid of her, though she talks so much and is so funny."

So the two retired.

And when they were alone Mrs. Winchell sat down and drew the poor frightened girl toward her by one hand, even made her partly sit on the somewhat refractory lap, from which a little dog even would have rolled off, borne down by gravitation. In a minute more Mrs. Winchell's arm was round Rachel's waist.

"So you are named Rachel, my dear. You do not know how natural that sounds. Why, I am named Lois myself." And then she laughed. "Not that that is anything to you. But you see I had an Aunt Lois, and she had a sister Rachel. They are both Bible names, you see, only one is Old Testament and one is New, you know."

"Yes, ma'am," faltered poor Rachel.

"And that is why 'Rachel' sounds natural, and that is what I meant to say. Now, don't you cry, dear. I know all about the sea. All of my father's people were seafaring people, and before I was married I always lived at Chatham. They are gone ever so long sometimes, but they turn up at last. Why, there was Captain Cobb, he sailed the Westmoreland. She was lost in the South Sea, and they all went ashore on the reef. And he had to go to Pitcairn's Island, and he had to build a schooner there; and he built it, and they came home—they all came home. He did not lose one man. But his wife—she was in mourning, and all the children were in mourning, and they had all been in mourning eight months—when one Sunday afternoon, just as meeting was over and they were coming out of the house, up drove a buggy from Brewster, and there was Captain Cobb as natural as ever, only a little stouter. They always turn up so. And you must not cry. But what is your other name?"

Rachel told her, and told her her father's plans in coming to America.

"Quite right, my dear; he is quite right. Why they do not all come I do not know, and never did. Well, when he comes we will send to Hitchin for him. Perhaps he will like to stay in Hitchin. All the young men go away. I am sure I do not know why. For there are good farms in Hitchin as I want to see. And if your father was only a blacksmith, why, Goodchild wants a striker badly; he said so to me Tuesday when I took Fanny there to be shod. Any way, I am glad he is coming to America. And your dear mother—how does she like the water? Is she sea-sick? Oh, I am horribly sea-sick when I go."

Poor Rachel put in a word edgewise to say that her mother was not so good a sailor as she. But Mrs. Winchell was already in full career.

"Miss Child thinks you had better come to Hitchin and wait. And I think so too. But you shall not come if you do not want to. Miss Child shall not manage you as she does me. You have some rights, my dear child, though I have none. She does as she chooses with me, but I will make a stout fight for you. Can you read, my dear child?"

"Why, of course I can read," said Rachel, amazed at the question.

"Yes, of course you can. But, you see, there is so much said about public education, and all that, how should I know? Read me this, my dear." And Mrs. Winchell took from her bag a volume of "The Standard Library."

With a very sweet voice—a low contralto—without the least nasal twang, with no sort of hesitation on the one side or pretence on the other, Rachel read a dozen lines from Mrs. Holloway's "Hours with Charlotte Brontë."

Mrs. Winchell listened, well pleased. "That is really the best thing of all," she said. "If you are good at finding lost spectacles, if you do that half as well as you read English, you will do very well for me. Hunting up spectacles, going to the door, and reading aloud in the evenings are the chief things I need of you. Can you drive a horse?"

"Why, no," said Rachel, startled. "Of course I cannot. At least I never tried."

Mrs. Winchell laughed heartily. "We will have you try. And you shall harness one too. No woman is independent till she can put a horse's collar and his harness on. I am afraid Mrs. Darusmont did not know that. But she will learn where she is now. They all mean well, and they will all learn. People who talk so much as they do must say a great many foolish things. But people who mean well will all learn.

"You will do for me very well, my poor dear little girl. But now comes the question, which is much more important, how well shall I do for you?

"You see what I look like. I am sixty years old, and I am rather fussy. I like to talk, and I do not like to be interrupted. I like to read, but my eyes are not what they were when I was fourteen. I like to give advice, and few people like to hear advice. I live eighty miles from here, in a quiet country town named Hitchin, as you heard me say. The men, as I tell you, all go away from it. All the more do the women do very much as they choose. I have time enough for my books, time enough for my chickens, time enough for my letters, time enough for my friends, time enough for my garden, when I can keep the chickens out of it. Life would be quite tolerable to me—my dear Rachel, is quite tolerable to me—but for two or three things. And those things make me come to Miss Child. And in these things she befriends me. First, as I tell you, I cannot read when I want to. I cannot or ought not to read in the evening at all. Second, as I tell you, or ought to tell you, I cannot keep the hens out of the garden. They are too quick for me. And for one hen I drive out I break down a dozen of my gladioluses. Third, both these burdens I could bear, and would bear, but that I lose my glasses. I lose them in all sorts of places. I buy a dozen pair at a time. I bought a dozen of Mr. Millar this morning, and they are in this bag now. But I can lose a dozen pair in two days. I can lose them faster than any one can find them. Mind me, dear child," said the old lady, laughing, "this is not my fault. Not at all. It is my constitution. I was born under that star, if you know what that means. The star of losing spectacles. Now you see whether I shall suit you. How should you like to spend a week, or two weeks, or three with an odd old lady who will be all the time sending you out of the house to drive the hens away from her flowers, and when you are not doing that will bid you get up and look for her spectacles ?"

Long before she had come thus far Rachel had been heart-drawn by the gentleness and tenderness of the old lady. And all her answer, sudden and without thought indeed, was given when, with eyes full, she said, "Thank you, so very much ; thank you. I shall be very pleased to go." And then with an impulse she could not account for Mrs. Winchell kissed the girl. Rachel was fully conscious that she had been eager, if she had dared, to kiss her new mistress.

The bargain was made. Miss Child herself did not dare ask on what terms when the two reappeared in her office, and when Mrs. Winchell told her that they had agreed.

"Have her at the Ladies' Room at the Maine Station at 3.40, is it ? I do not know when it is. But you will know my train."

CHAPTER IV.

HITCHIN.

" The sheltered cot, the cultivated farm,
The never-failing brook, the busy mill,
The decent church that topped the neighboring hill."
Deserted Village.

THE experience of riding by rail was almost a novelty to Rachel. In England an occasional little ride to her aunt's, and the long pull to Liverpool which had brought her to the fatal passage in the Baikal, were all the experiments of travel in her short life. And she did not find these precisely repeated, now that her experience of New-England began.

Miss Child herself took her to the station with her newly arranged luggage. Miss Child checked the trunk and valise, and gave the checks to Rachel with a little instruction on their uses. "Remember, my dear child, that they are your trunks. Put them in your pocket, and remember it is an ingenious invention by which you can carry your trunk in your pocket." Among forlorn women, and cheerful women, and women who constantly rose and looked out at the door, and other women who sat steadily and read "The Standard Library" and other approved serials, registered to go by mail in class No. 2, they sat, up to a moment which the careful Miss Child thought late, when Mrs. Winchell suddenly appeared, not flurried, but prompt, with a porter from the

Adams House, who evidently knew her and her eccentricities well.

"Here we are," she said. "Now, Leah, bid Miss Child good-by, and ask her to be as good a friend to you as she has been to me."

Poor sobbing Rachel needed no quickening. She was in the kind lady's arms, with the tears wetting the cheeks of both. It seemed to her a world of good-bys. No father, no mother, no Captain Ryland, no Mr. Wolff, and now, just as she knew this nice Miss Child, she must bid her good-by forever too.

"Do not mind, my dear girl, do not mind. Write me a letter sometimes, and if you want anything let me know." And the relentless porter, following obedient after Mrs. Winchell, led Rachel away.

"Drawing-room car?" asked the official on duty at the door of that palace.

"That depends. Have you two seats together on the east side? I shall not roast in the sun, nor my little girl here." And she looked at the ground plan of the palace. "You are sure you are going this way? You know if you once turn me round I will never ride in your old machine again. Eighteen? Seventeen? Yes, mark these two. Come here, Leah, come here. Good-by, dear Miss Child, good-by. I wish you would soon come and see how we live. Good-by, good-by." And then she took from the porter the last purchases— the new shawl for Rachel among other things—and who shall say how many wraps and hand-bags?

"Your checks is in the red Russia bag, mum," said the man as she tipped him. And she, as she turned to Rachel, "Leah, dear, try to remember that, for I shall forget. The checks are in the red Russia bag. That means that leather bag. You may keep that in your charge, Leah. That shall be your first responsibility. Now help me to find 17. I never can read their numbers in the darkness."

The girl was dazed and amazed. But a sense of humor helped her through, when she noticed the readiness with which a new country had given her a new name. She found numbers 17 and 18. Mrs. Winchell settled herself and her belongings, and at the instant the train passed into the open air.

And now Rachel screwed herself up to one great act of courage.

She certainly hoped to please this queer kind lady whose home was to be her place of work for three weeks or four. As for its being her own home, such a wild presumption never crossed Rachel's mind. She certainly did not want to offend her at the outset. But, without much reasoning, Rachel felt "in her bones," as Mrs. Winchell would have said, that if she were to lose her name because she was in strange clothes, in a strange house, in a strange land, she should lose everything. That was all she had left to stand by. And, with a divine instinct, Rachel understood that the matter of name was no trifle.

Mrs. Winchell looked serenely on the bay as the train swept across the bridge, with nothing which suggested any desire for conversation. In fact, she was going back in a hasty review of the day to see if she had done three things which she ought to have done, and if she had not left undone three and thirty.

"Please, Mrs. Winchell," said Rachel boldly, "would you be good enough, when you speak to me, to call me Rachel?"

"My dear little Leah, of course I will, of course I will. I beg your pardon twenty thousand times. My poor little Leah, you are not ill-favored at all. But how shall I ever remember? The very first moment Miss Child said your name was Rachel—no, you said so yourself—my Aunt Leah crossed the canvas, as our dear Mr. Primrose would say, and from that moment that became your name. But, dear child, do not be frightened. You shall not lose your name. How ever shall we manage it?

"I will tell you, Leah.

"Whenever I call you Leah, remember, you shall not answer me.'

And so, in what did not seem a long three hours, they found themselves in Hitchin. There was not one point in the ride from the railway station to Mrs. Winchell's comfortable old-fashioned mansion which resembled Rachel's experience when she had made her annual visit to her English aunt at the seaside. The carriage in which they rode was different, the trees by the wayside were different, the terrace in front of the house was different, the steps to the front door were different.

When they entered, the rooms were different, the furniture was different; but Mrs. Winchell was as kind as her Aunt Ann would have been to Rachel, was quite as kind as any aunts could have been, and the child was as hungry as she had ever been in her life.

If she had but known it, indeed, she was as tired. She had gone through, in one day, experiences as varied as some people extend over a lifetime.

"Your bed is the place for you, dear Leah," said Mrs. Winchell, and this time poor Rachel had neither heart nor strength to make any battle with her.

She had hardly more than a chance to see how pretty and pleasant was her bedroom, and then, with the happy omnipotence of girlhood, she fell asleep and slept, without turning on her pillow, till morning.

It was not till the morning was nearly over that the impending battle came. As Rachel dressed herself she had been only too sure that it must come. She was not quarrelsome, but she had girded herself to it. She must meet the enemy—no, dear kind old Mrs. Winchell was not her enemy, but she must meet her in fair field, though she had not either stone or sling.

The girl would not lose her name. She had lost her country, her ship, her clothing, her books — her place in the world she had lost. Perhaps, as the reader knows, she had lost her father and her mother. But Rachel would not say that, even to herself; nay, was not even troubled by the thought. So easy had been her own boat voyage, that it was not easy for her to think the others fared worse. Still, the other realities of life she had lost. And for the time she had lost father and mother. She had nothing left to her but her name.

"That I cannot lose," said Rachel aloud, as she brushed her hair in front of the pretty looking-glass, sitting at the pretty dressing-table of her room.

"That I cannot lose." And then the girl remembered how her cousin Martha, who was a little stage-struck, used to spout:

> "He that filches from me my good name,
> Robs me of that which not enriches him,
> And makes me poor indeed."

So Rachel went down-stairs girt for battle.

But, as usual, when one is all ready for battle, battle did not come.

We used to read in those too dull histories at school that Marshal Daun drew out his army and offered battle, but that Marshal Kraun refused. And so it was here. Breakfast passed without a breeze, and Rachel learned the names of ten articles of food she had never seen before. Then she helped Mrs. Winchell, as she washed the cups and saucers and put them away. She went into the garden with her, and cut the flowers. She walked from room to room with her in her daily progress, and gradually learned the names of the red parlor and the green parlor, the colonel's room, and the chamber in the ell. She held a skein of yarn while Mrs. Winchell wound it. She received careful instruction about Van Stan's stratena, and held the bottle while Mrs. Winchell mended the broken head of a Venus de Milo which had been knocked down in her absence. She was taught the difference between this cement and liquid glue—when she was to use the one and when the other.

But in all this there was never a moment for battle. Nay, Rachel even forgot that she was girt for battle.

But there was one moment which reminded her that the cloud still threatened.

"No, my dear child, you had better not call me Mrs. Winchell. Very few people whom I like call me Mrs. Winchell. Even Mr. Tyndale calls me Aunt Lois. And I like you, my dear child, so you will call me Aunt Lois—if you like to," she added almost fearfully, as if she might have gone too far.

"If I like to!" cried Rachel, with the tears in her eyes; "of course I like to." And at that moment the thought of battle crossed her mind, and it seemed like an ugly dream, and all her grand resolves to be the wild delirium of rebellion.

But all the same the cloud burst and the shock came.

And the air was the clearer after it was over.

The morning mail had come. Mrs. Winchell had

extended herself on her sofa to read her *Advertiser*. "Let us see what Mr. Hale says," she said, as she opened the paper, though it was twenty years since Mr. Hale had been its editor. She had given to Rachel Miss Alcott's "Little Women," and Rachel was absorbed for the first time in the luxury of the companionship of those estimable persons.

Half an hour passed quietly when Mrs. Winchell was called into the hall to see a man who had maps of Palestine to sell. She disposed of him by giving to him two pictures of Jerusalem, a cup of coffee and a slice of bread and butter, and a chromolith of the mosque at Delhi. She explained to him that he was never under any circumstances to come to that house again.

The man departed, and the old lady returned to her sofa and her newspaper. But her spectacles were nowhere to be found.

"What have I done with my glasses?" she cried. "Leah, my child, now your real duties have begun; look in the hall, look on the mat, and see where I have laid those things."

But Rachel never lifted an eyelid or moved a muscle.

"Leah, Leah!" cried the old lady, impatiently. "Don't you hear me? I have lost my glasses, and I am miserable without them."

But Rachel never stirred.

"Can this child be hard of hearing?" said Aunt Lois aloud; "how strange that I have never noticed it before." And a sort of horror came over her at the suspicion that she was losing her own quickness of perception. The other fear, that she had imported an incompetent assistant into the household, scarcely crossed her unselfish mind.

She crossed to where the girl sat, touched her on the

shoulder, and in a loud tone, as if she were calling to a workman at the other end of the garden, she cried slowly and very distinctly, "My dear child, I have lost my glasses."

Rachel sprang to her feet, and in a moment brought them back to the wondering old lady. "Here they are, dear Aunt Lois," she said, blushing but fearless.

It was the first time she had used the familiar title of endearment. "I am not deaf; I heard you speak both times before. But it seemed as if you were speaking to your father's sister, though I did not see her here."

"You are a little witch," cried Aunt Lois, more in admiration than in anger, and she stooped and kissed the child, who was by this time frightened at her own courage.

Aunt Lois was not given to kissing, and the victory was won.

CHAPTER V.

THE DEMANDS OF SOCIETY.

"Right well she knew, each temper to descry,
To thwart the proud and the submiss to raise."
Shenstone.

"RACHEL," said Mrs. Winchell on the second morning, "I have quite settled it in the night that you shall go to school."

"Yes, ma'am."

But poor Rachel's heart sank as she said, "Yes, ma'am." For going to school in a strange land, among these strange-looking girls, seemed almost like falling into the sea to be pulled out by another set of boat-hooks. And it seemed again like permanency in Ilitchin, while she had all along supposed that she was here, as it were, only on a visit of a few weeks, until the glad despatch should come telling her in which part of the world her father and mother had landed. So it was with a big lump in her throat that Rachel assented.

Mrs. Winchell was quick enough to catch the tone of the girl's feeling, and quick enough to address it on the instant.

"You see, my dear child, it is only the summer school, and it will only last two or three weeks more. You will not learn anything—at least anything to speak of. But you will see the other girls, and that will be better for you than to be shut up with an old woman here all the time." And after a pause: "It is something to see and hear Hannah Cate, and be near her."

"Seeing the other girls" was the last thing to recommend the new enterprise to poor Rachel. What little she had seen of other girls had only impressed her with profound terror since she had been in America. There had been a group of other girls hanging round the railroad station when she and her mistress left the train. And Rachel had shrunk with horror from their keen investigation of her and her belongings. Why they were there at all was a mystery to her. Had they no mothers or fathers, or possibly no homes?

But Rachel did not dare say a single word in reply to Mrs. Winchell. If she were to go to school, to school she would go, and she would pray God, as she had so often, that she might do her duty in the place of life to which He should be pleased to call her.

Only in her carnal heart she did wish that He had not been pleased to call her to the summer school of District No. 11.

District No. 11. For, as it happened, by good fortune or ill fortune, Mrs. Winchell lived just without the magic line of the "Centre District." Had Rachel and Mrs. Winchell lived inside this line, Rachel would have had but a short walk to the Centre School, and she would have had certain facilities for education which to the Centre School belonged. But, as it happened, the line ran just on the other side of Mrs. Winchell's barn, and so Rachel had every morning a walk of three quarters of a mile out in the open country to the school-house of District No. 11. The school kept here—if one use the slang of the profession—was not a graded school; it was a district school, and received all comers from a-b-c-darians at the one hand to curious inquirers into binomial theorems on the other. Over all comers Miss Hannah Cate presided.

Mrs. Winchell had the wit and knowledge of affairs to address a note to Miss Hannah, in which she told her of her new pupil, and asked her to take tea that evening, that teacher and pupil might be the better acquainted. This note was intrusted to a barefoot boy, who was intercepted for this purpose on his way to school at the Five Corners, and by a miracle the boy remembered to deliver the note before the morning school was over. Accordingly Miss Hannah appeared after the afternoon session, and was made cordially welcome.

Rachel saw in an instant that all was well. Here was no she-dragon with a rod in one hand and a slate in the other, glowering angrily through green spectacles, as Rachel's too ready fancy had pictured from the first moment. A slight, fair, tall, pretty girl, very simply dressed, but nicely dressed, met Rachel at far more than half way, and captivated her in a moment. Miss Hannah had pinned in the waist of her dress two or three spikes of cardinal flowers, which were the earliest of the season. One of the big boys had brought them, in homage to her, and they had been kept fresh all day. They were the first Rachel ever saw, and she never in her life saw another but she thought of dear Miss Hannah.

So this was the ogre into whose hands she was to be delivered the next morning.

"Dear Aunt Lois, how good for you to send for me. And I have stretched your invitation. I went home at noon and brought my brush and comb and all my things, and I am going to spend the night with you. Then I can take Rachel to school in the morning, and she will not be afraid."

Half the load was lifted from poor Rachel already. But was this really the schoolmistress? Why, she was only a little taller than Rachel's Cousin Polly in Haworth, and she did not look a day older. Rachel was not afraid of Polly at all. They always spent the summer together at Aunt Ann's. Was it possible that she should be no more afraid of Miss Hannah than she was of Cousin Polly?

Possible it was, and so it proved.

From that beginning the school was never a terror, but a simple joy. They walked to the school-house the next morning with a train of coadjutors, increasing with every house they passed, till a troop of ten or eleven entered together. The two who held Miss Hannah's hand were in highest honor, and on this sacred occasion Rachel was one of the two. Queer the children were to her, and mysterious their costumes. Most of the girls had pink sun-bonnets made from pasteboard and calico. The boys invariably had worn palm-leaf hats much broken at the edges. Most of the girls had shoes. None of the boys had. The lack was not a sign of poverty, but of independence. Shoes would have controlled the freedom of action of their feet as much as white kid gloves would have interfered with the uses to which they meant to put their hands. They left both to occasions of more ceremony.

Once in the school-room all parties accepted, as of course, a system of more restraint. Pink bonnets and straw hats were hung in a little porch or propylæum, and teacher and scholars entered the square white room, with windows wherever windows were possible, which was consecrated to learning. Forms of pine wood, much adorned by the carvings of a generation, gave two seats each to boys and girls. The whole company, including

Miss Hannah, were not twenty. Precisely at nine she struck her bell; all was hushed, and she read a few verses from the Bible and repeated the Lord's Prayer. Then the girl led the children in singing "Ward," and with perfect good order they all joined in two verses of a hymn. Miss Hannah gave her orders to the others, which were obeyed with absolute precision, and then she smiled and beckoned to the " new girl."

And poor Rachel was by no means disgraced in her first examination. It proved that there were certain matters which she and Jane Dyer and Relief Vincent could study together. Certain other matters Rachel was to do alone. In such matters as a b ab, she was sent out on the roadside with Tommy Cashman and Huldah Furness to quicken their halting memories. She had brought a new copy-book with her, and Miss Hannah, who despised the engraved copies, set her a line to copy.

"An amiable aunt answers all appeals."

Despite the queer pronunciation and the geography before unheard of, Rachel soon found that school is school, and her morning sped by more quickly and serenely than she could have believed.

And when twelve came, and the moment of emancipation, Rachel was surprised to think she was so wholly at home.

"Dear Miss Hannah," cried Relief eagerly, "to-day you will stay with us. I know you will. You know you said you would stay one day this week. And I got up early this morning, and see here, I baked all these biscuits myself all on purpose, Miss Hannah. Oh, Miss Hannah, it will be a shame if you do not stay!"

And great hulking Tom Henderson now produced from a cool place in the brook a tin can containing two or three quarts of thimbleberries, which he had brought in the determination that Miss Hannah should stay. Pies, doughnuts, cheese, even two baked custards were produced, as additions to the regale, all which helped to make the invitation more irresistible. And Jane added to it, in a sheepish way, the request, "Ask her, Miss Hannah, if she won't stay too."

And when it was decided that Miss Hannah would stay, just for this once, through the two hours' intermission, the victory was celebrated with enthusiasm. Rachel entered quite into the spirit of the picnic. She was only sorry she had contributed nothing. But now it appeared that Miss Hannah was not unprepared, and that Mrs. Winchell had stored her bag with such bonbons for a dessert that she and Rachel were by no means beggars at the common feast.

This jolly lunch spread on the teacher's table and the forms of the school-house cemented Rachel's relations with all the "other girls." When she went home at night she told Mrs. Winchell that she could not thank her enough for sending her to school, and that she would never be afraid again of anything she proposed for her.

The truth was, that these summer days, which Rachel supposed were to be only a queer little episode in the beginning of her new American life, which she knew must be wholly unlike her life with her father and her mother, were striking for her the keynote of it all. As it proved, there were to be more than ten of these days—more than twenty, more than thirty. After a little it was clear that the ocean fleet of boats from the Baikal had not been relieved by any steamer for America. After a little more it became only too clear that no steamer for England had picked them up. One day, about a fortnight after Rachel's arrival, Mr. Tyndale, the minister, came in with his newspaper in his hand, and then he was closeted with Mrs. Winchell for half an hour. Afterward he came in every day so soon as the mail arrived at Hitchin, and there was a longer or shorter private interview. But it was not till more than a month after Rachel's arrival in Boston that she was summoned into the "colonel's room," where these private conferences took place, and then, with all possible kindness, Aunt Lois told the sobbing girl that there was no reason whatever to think that the lost boats could ever be found. Not one of them had ever been heard of, and the resources of conjecture had been given up.

In fact, Mr. Tyndale had heard from his correspondents in New York that the life companies there had already received notifications of the death of people on the Baikal, from friends who had given up all hope and wished to adjust the estates of the shipwrecked men and women.

Aunt Lois was all kindness in her rapid, eager way.

"You are here, dear child. That is one thing. A great rule in life is to stay where you are until a door opens. You do not see any open door, and I do not. Till a door opens you will stay here. You see"—with an attempt at a smile—"I am your guardian for the moment. I must tell you what to do. You will stay here, and you will pick up my spectacles, and hold my yarn, and drive away the hens for me, till some other mission opens, dear girl. You know, my child, you know how poor Aunt Lois would miss you if you were not here." Thus she chattered on, fairly dreading the depth of the child's grief if neither of them said anything. And she made poor Rachel bend over from the arm of the chair in which she sat and cry upon her shoulder.

And Mr. Tyndale prudently went away.

Then there was correspondence with Aunt Ann—correspondence which Rachel hated. She liked Aunt Ann and her Cousin Sarah, but she was well aware that she had no wish to return to England to go to them to live; indeed, she had already imbibed so much of the New Englander's spirit that she saw no reason why she should. They did not want to have her come, and she did not want to go. That, in Rachel's mind, settled the thing. Nor did Aunt Lois take much interest in the correspondence.

"It is Fetich, my child; it is all Fetich," said the queer old lady. "It is the ancient Fetich known as '*Respectability*' whom we worship. There were times when the clan was everything, and the clan had to be held together. And because of those times, in these times, which are very different, I am expected to obey the old Fetich law. Why, last week my husband's second cousin was killed in a fight in Denver. I do not know that he was not drunk when he died. I do not know if he was. I do not know anything about him. But I do know that because Richard the First lived in the feudal system I was expected to put a black ribbon on my bonnet when the Hon. George Winchell, Mayor of Diggsville, was shot in Denver. I did not do it, my child. I would not render this homage to the great Fetich. But I do it now. I bend my proud knees, and I write this letter to your Aunt Ann, who does not love you half as much as I do, so that the decencies inherited from the feudal system may be properly observed."

Rachel hardly understood what her Aunt Ann had to do with the fate of the Mayor of Diggsville, but she said meekly, "Aunt Ann is very nice and very kind."

"My dear, I know that. Anybody you had spent a

summer with would be nice and kind, let alone spending two or three since you were a little girl.

"But that is no reason—none, Rachel—why she should call you back over the seas and make you take again, alone, this horrible risk, merely that she and you and I may perform Baal worship before the altar of the great Dagon idol of Respectability.

"Let Aunt Ann be supreme on her side of the water, and let me be supreme on mine."

Mrs. Winchell need not have distressed herself. Aunt Ann was perhaps more of a worshipper of the great Fetich of Respectability than Aunt Lois. But Aunt Ann lived in the outskirts of a half-fashionable watering-place, where she knew to a shilling how much a year's life cost for her and her daughter Sarah. She knew to a shilling how much dear Rachel's bread and butter and jam and mutton would cost, how much her schooling would cost, and her frocks, and bonnets, and shoes, and shawls, and cloaks. She knew how long it would be before Rachel would earn anything even if she rose to the rank of a governess. She knew how long it would be before she would have any chance to degrade herself to the rank of assistant book-keeper in the well-known establishment of Shoolbred & Fettyplace. Aunt Ann therefore wrote a letter—not cordial, though it was meant to be not cool. It intimated quite distinctly that the original voyage was not her plan; that her sister and brother had undertaken it in face of her counsels. It did not say that the sins and imprudences of the parents must descend upon the child, but it implied as much. Then, lightly waiving the theological question thus suggested, the letter said that to return to the practical question, perhaps it would be best to decide nothing now. While there was life there would always be hope, Aunt Ann said, though what that remark had to do with the matter in hand she did not say. And as, before Rachel could sail for home the critical period of the equinoxial storm would be at hand (Aunt Ann prided herself on the "equinoxial storm" as a masterpiece, spelling and all),—as Rachel seemed to be now with dear Christian friends, Aunt Ann ventured to take the responsibility of leaving the whole decision to those friends, knowing that in any event Rachel would be a good girl, and acquiesce in her aunt's decision as made from the best motives, and try to do her duty in the condition of life into which it should please God to place her.

Rachel read this letter twice, and gave it silently to Aunt Lois, who was waiting with a good deal of anxiety. She read it once only.

"What does she mean, Rachel? You ought to know her better than I."

"Dear Aunt Lois," cried the girl, flinging her head into the old lady's lap, "she means that she does not want me living with her, but that she is ashamed to say so.

"Do not think hardly of her, dear Aunt Lois. You do not know how hard she has to pinch to keep inside the lines of—well, of the class of life she lives in.

"She does love me, Aunt Lois. If I were there she would never send me away.

"But"—here she smiled so prettily on Aunt Lois— "but I am not there."

"Thank God for that, my child," said Aunt Lois resolutely. And she put her arm round her neck and patted her and petted her. "How lucky about the equinoctial! and this year I believe it will blow much longer than usual. I am quite sure I would not trust it before the next equinoctial comes. Rachel, you shall write her a pretty note. You shall say that the queer old lady in whose house you are is under certain circumstances greatly in danger of neuralgia complicated by rheumatism and coupled by constitutional predisposition. Say that the person in whose opinion she has most confidence, and you, recommend decidedly that in the present contingency she shall not risk the chances of a change of a personal attendant, and that justly weighing this unbiassed advice she is sure, and you believe, that it is your duty as now advised to remain in Hitchin, unless your aunt sees super—superanything considerations which may outweigh these conclusions.

"Say something like that, child. Write large, so as to cover four pages of paper. If there is any trouble about the long words, take Worcester's Dictionary. One word is about as good as another, if it is only long enough. Thus shall we pay fit homage to the Fetich."

Then, seeing that Rachel was really troubled, "Dear child, do not cry; your other aunt is right. It is nonsense to determine anything. Only God determines anything, and sometimes I think He does not care much about time. If you can see three months ahead in life you need never bother yourself to look further.

"Now of one thing we are sure—I love you and you love me."

"Yes, ma'am," said the grateful Rachel, with her eyes full of tears.

"There, then, is one bit of Eternity. For love is eternal.

"Of that bit of eternity we take one little sliver, and we say, 'This is certain, that Rachel lives with Aunt Lois till, because they love each other, it shall be better for one of them to go away.'"

And in fact a letter was written to Aunt Ann, and re-written. It was altered and copied, and altered again.

But, substantially on the lines of Aunt Lois's original sketch, it went to England, and answered every available purpose.

CHAPTER VI.

GAYETY AND CHARITY.

"A LITTLE pebble dropped into a stream
  Sends lovely widening circles out, and then
Far upward, till the water and the air
  Are full of life beyond our thought and ken."
                                                      Miss C. Dugan.

MEANWHILE Aunt Lois sent for Miss Blaney, the dressmaker, and Miss Blaney took some requisite measures of Rachel's form and figure. A sufficient order was given to Miss Blaney to keep her busy for a month and to satisfy the Hitchin respect for home industries. For the rest a liberal order was sent to Hovey, in Boston, and so in a few weeks' time Rachel was as nicely dressed as Aunt Lois's daughter would have been dressed; and in fact she assumed in the household much the same place as a niece or granddaughter of her age might have done.

So soon as the finery was in proper order Mrs. Winchell selected the occasion for its first use.

"Rachel, my child," she said, "Nahum is off duty. He has begged leave to go to Great Falls to see his grandmother buried, I believe, or her grandson married. Indeed, I do not know which. The family at Great Falls is past finding out. Seven grandmothers have died there since Nahum lived with me, I am sure; but I ask no questions.

"Nahum has gone to Great Falls. So you must step to the front.

"Do not be frightened. There is no wood to cut and no pig to kill. But you will have to drive me over to Mrs. Barnard's to the Sewing Circle."

Rachel asked nothing better. Many of the other girls of their region were going. The Sewing Circle was most democratic in its range, and swept in all social conditions, so people only could and would sew for the poor, and it was most indifferent as to ages. Old Madam Fuller always went in fine weather, and she remembered the first "progress" of Washington, who on that occasion had kissed his hand to her personally. On the other hand, they were glad to get in as many young girls as they could, if it were only to have them carry round the tea and coffee and bread and butter. Besides, it "interested them" early in life. Such was the excuse, and the people of Hitchin were right. Nothing is better for boy or girl than to be counted into the working force of the world early.

So when Nahum left for the funeral of his grandmother he left Kate, the mare, harnessed in her stall, and all that Rachel and Hitty had to do in the afternoon was to lead her out and put her into Mrs. Winchell's own buggy, a feat for which they were quite prepared. Rachel was quite clear about her skill in driving.

"When Nahum comes home from the funeral, Rachel," said the old lady, so soon as they were well adjusted, "he shall teach you the whole art and mystery of harnessing. The wonder is how they put on the collar, and the difficulty is to slip the bit into a hollow channel there is among their teeth. The miracle is, my dear Rachel—one of the marvellous adaptations of nature, as Parson Caner would call it—that horses have not the slightest carnivorous disposition. If they had, they would bite off the thumbs of the men who try to bit them every day, and with that savory morsel would go gambolling in the paddock. Curious, that similarity between the words 'to bite' and 'to bit.' Note that, Rachel, and ask Miss Cate to look in Marsh's Wedgwood about it. For the present, remember that the independence of woman consists in three things :

"First, she must be able to harness her own horse. If she can, all the men may go to their grandmothers' funerals.

"Second, she must have an india-rubber cloak which will go down to her heels.

"Third, she must have india-rubber boots which shall go up to her knees.

"If she have these, why, she can go to her own grandfather's funeral, even if it rains cats and dogs, as at funerals I think it is apt to do."

Mrs. Barnard received the visitors most cordially on the hospitable Greek portico which screened the front of her house, which was the grandest house in the West Village, as Mrs. Winchell's was perhaps the grandest near the East. And a pretty party was that which now went forward. The whole house was flung open to the army of charity skirmishers. They formed by threes or by fours, in squads of tens or twenty, if need were, or even in companies, well disciplined, which could have displayed a company front of fifty had there been any need. They were scattered in this summer house, and on that piazza, in the great parlor, or the summer parlor, or the library, or the breakfast-room, as fancy or accident directed, and everybody took the skirmisher's privilege of changing the point of attack against the unseen enemy — nay, of changing the weapon employed whenever she chose.

The unseen enemy was the devil, whom the Sewing Circle of Hitchin had bravely undertaken to overthrow by any means in its power. And truly, to a person not a theologian, it would have seemed that on this occasion the society had succeeded, and that he had betaken himself to his " cressets of burning naphtha." Let us hope that the Patent Law restricts him from using General Rosecrans's magnificent invention of burning naphtha with the strong draught of glass tubes, and that he and his defeated army are compelled to use their naphtha smoking as well as blazing. Certainly, in the garden of Mrs. Barnard's, and in her airy parlors, his appearance was most subtly concealed, if he were there at all.

The one difficulty of the managers of the Sewing Society was to know to what end their labors, if those were labors which gave all pleasure and which fatigued no one, should be directed. And on this occasion, when the setting of a luxurious supper had called into the house all stragglers, and the larger part of the company, including all who were of authority, had assembled in Mrs. Barnard's immense summer parlor, the question was brought up in form what object of philanthropy should be selected for the next three months. The minister's wife, a jolly little woman, presided, or was said to preside. But in fact her hands were upheld, as her husband would have said, by Mrs. Barnard on the one side and Mrs. Winchell on the other. And the proceedings, though clogged a good deal by talk of " laying on the table," and " amending," and " accepting" this and that report of this or that committee, bore no close resemblance to those of any constitutional legislature.

None the less, however, did they attain their end, and that very directly.

There was nobody who could be called a subject for charity in the town except Elder Faunce, so called, and his wife, who had many years ago expressed their preference to reside in the poorhouse, an old inn on the North Road which the town had bought when staging died out, and which was, in fact, kept by Elder Faunce's nephew. He received it from the town with the understanding that he was to make what he could off the farm, and the town paid him two hundred dollars a year for living in such an unpromising place. He would otherwise have been raising wheat in Illinois. A committee of the ladies visited this town farm every second Sunday and conducted religious service there, and on Fast Day and Thanksgiving another committee revised the wardrobe of the Elder and his wife. The Elder was called "Elder" not from any ecclesiastical function which he had ever exercised, but because he was in fact the oldest man in the town, having been named Rochambeau Faunce in honor of the surrender at Yorktown, the week after the news of that event arrived in Hitchin. For the rest, at Thanksgiving time a small canister of tea generally appeared at old Miss Fosdick's by express, and nobody knew where it came from. And sometimes in a similar way a piece of shirting appeared at the Widow Millmore's. But nobody said that these things were connected with the item, "Buttons, pins, needles, and other sundries," in the annual report of Miss Willard, the treasurer of the Sewing Society.

It would not have been agreeable either to the Widow Millmore or to Miss Fosdick, both of whom would be present among the co-operative circle in the annual meeting, to hear the precise cost of the tea or of the shirting. In fact, each of these ladies supposed that these articles came from old admirers who had risen to the topmost round of the ladder of success in Boston.

The poor of the town, such as they were, having been thus disposed of, the Sewing Circle had other worlds to conquer. On this occasion a letter was read from a church in Elba, in Washington Territory, which was about to hold a fair for the purchase of a carpet, and which asked the assistance of the "friends in Hitchin." But this letter only awakened laughter in the company. The truth was that it had no voucher, and had only been written because the Elba people had seen in the *Independent* that Hitchin had helped a "struggling church" in Colorado. The next appeal had been directed to that jolly, good-natured Miss Sharpe, who was sitting and knitting in the bow-window.

"Will you read the letter yourself, Miss Sharpe?"

"Oh, no, Miss Willard—you read so well."

So Miss Willard, in good academical style, declaimed the letter. Miss Sharpe said she had not seen the writer since they were all at school together at Kearsarge, but that she liked her then, and thought she was good and genuine. The letter said that by a strange fortune of war or of peace the writer had been left, on the close of hostilities, literally the owner of a plantation on an island off the coast of North Carolina. The estate had first been confiscated, then the owner and his sons had been killed in war, and the Missionary Society which supported her had bought the title from the heir-at-law. The Missionary Society had blown up, but the writer was there with a great school of boys and girls of all colors, whose old industries, such as they were, were broken up by the war and the peace, and to whom, after four or five years of confusion, she was trying to teach the arts of peace. She was teaching the girls how to knit and the long-legged boys how to dredge for oysters.

"I do not pretend that I shall give to them the clothing you may choose to send me. I shall sell it to them, or give it to them in payment for their work. But their work will, in its way, build up Jerusalem."

This sort of work pleased the maids and matrons of Hitchin. And to this and similar enterprises they gave their approval, not by any formal vote, but by a sort of buzz of conversation which, as the Friends would say, intimated distinctly enough what was "the sense of the meeting."

It was when the business meeting, so called, was well over, when the brothers, and husbands, and fathers, and sons, and possibly the "pretenders" and "lovers" of the ladies present began to come in, and to lounge round among the workwomen, that, with them, Satan entered also.

At least it was in an incident which then transpired that Rachel saw the only flash of his spear which she did see that evening.

She was sitting with Ruth Cordis by Miss Willard, the treasurer, a somewhat dried-up, not to say starched and insular person, a "considerably old-looking young lady." Mr. Thomas Poore came up, and with his cup of coffee took a seat by them.

"Miss Willard, they tell me you are the treasurer," he said.

"Yes, I have that honor," said the Argus of the treasury, laughing.

"Have you much difficulty in your investments?"

"None at all," said she. "We lend to the Lord, and the dividends are enormous."

"That encourages me," he said. "I was lured on

to-day, by my good nature, in Boston, to make a purchase of stock. Now it has occurred to me that it is much more in your line than in mine, and I will unload, as the Wall Street men say—I will present it all to the Sewing Society."

Miss Willard supposed that this was a joke, as indeed it was, and did not show any undue eagerness or gratitude.

Rachel was astonished at her indifference indeed, which in any other part of the world would have proved underbreeding. But Rachel did not know New England.

"Pray, what will you give us?" said Miss Willard, as if the society received a dozen gold nuggets at every meeting.

"I shall give you what Dr. Johnson called 'the potentiality of untold wealth.' Williams, who is an old classmate of mine, 'stuck me' to-day with three shares of a corporation of which he is president.

"It is the New England Stocking-Loom corporation, and has the exclusive right for New England to make and sell the new stocking-loom which is to put an end to all such industries as these young ladies are now pursuing. As I say, this is much more in your line than it is in mine. The shares cost me two dollars and a half apiece, and I will present all three to the Sewing Society."

The young man thought he had done a good-natured thing. He did not think he had done a rude thing.

But at this moment Satan entered Miss Willard. No lesser power could have inspired her rude reply:

"Oh, I see. Your friend was afraid of his stock, and put it on you; and you are afraid. 'Individual liability,' you gentlemen call it, do you not? and you want to put it on our broad shoulders."

Rachel did not understand all the ineffable rudeness of this speech, but she did know that it was rude. Ruth Cordis blushed crimson, she was so angry.

But Mr. Poore showed no mark of anger. Perhaps he knew Miss Willard too well. He only laughed.

"What, not accept my humble flower?" he said. "Then I will divide my bouquet into three. Miss Ruth, will you accept a share in the Stocking Loom? You do not know how many millions of children in Timbuctoo it will fit out with good red yarn stockings before it eats its breakfast. Indeed, I believe it runs all night if the water-wheel runs, and never eats any breakfast at all."

"Of course I will, Mr. Poore, and I will thank you to boot. I do not look a gift stocking-loom in the mouth."

Satan had by this time entered Miss Cordis, and this was her side hit at Miss Willard.

"And will this young lady take one share?" asked Mr. Poore.

Rachel was afraid. She did not want to offend anybody. She did not want to accept presents from strangers; but clearly this was half nonsense and was all a trifle, so she blushed very prettily, and thanked Mr. Poore, and took the share.

"And I will keep the third," said he, "and when we meet at Tiffany's to invest our profits in diamonds, we will send a little brooch to Miss Willard here to make her repent that she rejected our offer. I will send you the certificates to-morrow," he said, and so finished his coffee and took the cup back to Mrs. Barnard.

Miss Willard was wondering whether she had acted like a fool.

Mr. Poore was not wondering at all on that matter.

As soon as Rachel was in the wagon with Aunt Lois she told her story, and asked what she should have done.

The old lady was amused and indignant at the right points.

"You did quite right, my dear.

"In such a thing as this, if you have a set of right principles at bottom, you cannot go far wrong.

"That Miss Willard is a fool.

"If he sends you the certificate, well; it is not worth the postage-stamp on his letter.

"If he forgets all about it, well, too.

"You did perfectly right, Rachel. I am glad you like Ruth Cordis. She is a pet of mine."

Mr. Poore did not forget all about it. Next morning the elegantly engraved certificate of stock came, and had been properly transferred, the indorsement said, to Miss Rachel Finley.

"Put it in the bottom of the little desk," said Aunt Lois. "It will be a good thing to remember Mrs. Barnard by."

CHAPTER VII.

ANOTHER NEW WORLD.

"In each we sat, we heard the grave professor."
Princess.

But it is not for this little book to attempt to describe in such detail the fortunes of Hitchin, its gossip or its work, its ups or its downs, during the years of Rachel's first stay there. They were years quite as eventful as any which had passed in its history in the hundred and fifty years since the two Norcross brothers, in their lumber-prospecting, had lighted on the valley, had built two log-cabins there, and had brought to them their wives and their children. Quite as eventful were these years, and not more so.

In three such years, eventful or uneventful according to the standard by which one measures events, Rachel lived with Aunt Lois, as she began. A healthy, well-balanced life it was, with enough of sensation and not too much, enough of duty and not too much, enough of play and not too much. In that house there were plenty of books and not too many, there were enough people and not too many. Half the year, or about half the year, Rachel went to school. Mrs. Winchell would as soon have fired a pistol-ball through her head as to send her to school for more than six months in the year at her age; and, as it happened, the good sense of the average New Hampshire custom had drifted into that arrangement. There was a three-months school in winter and a three-months school in summer. At neither was the pace very fast nor the strain or drain on life very exhausting. When time came Rachel was transferred from the district school, which has been described, to the High School, which for all scholars over the age of fifteen was kept in "the Centre."

Mrs. Winchell was perfectly indifferent to the school requisitions of attendance, except that of promptness when the day's work began. "You must keep your appointments, Rachel. That young woman is there at nine to teach you. You must be there at nine to be taught, if you are there at all. That is the contract." But it was not in the contract that Rachel should go if Mrs. Winchell thought there was anything better for her.

"That is for me to say, my dear, not for them. I pay my taxes, and I pay them willingly. I should pay them if I had no chick nor child, and I should pay them willingly. But I have never contracted that you should be there every day."

So, if there were a good concert troupe in Boston Mrs. Winchell would pack up, at an hour's notice after she had read the announcement in the newspaper, and take Rachel with her for a week to the Adams House, that they might go to the entertainment.

"I am sorry for the others, my dear; I should be glad if I could take them all. But that I cannot do. As it is, I do what I can, and Miss What's-her-name must not expect that she is to be your only teacher. There is a great deal to be learned at places of amusement, if you only go to work the right way."

Nor was the old lady very particular as to her choice of the books which she made Rachel read aloud to her.

There was nothing she did not dip into. "I never said I understood it, my dear, and I never pretended to. But I did not mean that anybody else should select my reading for me." This was when she had sent down for somebody's treatise on the correlation of forces, which proved to be a little beyond her comprehension, or Rachel's.

"We know now, my dear child, that that is not in our line. How should we know, had we never tried?"

And if any one else pleaded with her in poor Rachel's behalf, and said it was impossible that a girl of that age could be interested in Tylor's "Anthropology :"

"My dear, I never said she should be interested. The good God never said she should be interested. As Mr. Carlyle has it, there is no act of Parliament that she should be interested. She will have, before she is done, to do a great many things that are not interesting, and to see a great many uninteresting people. Depend upon it, Sarah, she will pull through such experiences the better if she has a few doses of my good tonic wormwood now. Tylor's 'Anthropology' is her wormwood."

For Rachel herself, she would have said that her life was thoroughly happy. She was no fool, and she had, either by inheritance or by contagion from Mrs. Winchell, sense enough to make herself mistress of circumstances, and she had taken on, before she knew it, the habit of laughing at people who want to live in a world of sugar-candy.

But even Aunt Lois's optimism did not think this could last forever.

They had been spending the last weeks of August and the first of September at Waterville, to sensible people one of the pleasantest tarrying-places in the White Mountains. The day after their return, when the trunks were all unpacked, and they were both trying to take on home habits again, Aunt Lois said to Rachel:

"Come here, my child; there, sit just there.

"Rachel, Hitchin is a good place, but, as Mr. Lowell says of Judee, they don't know everything, not even in Hitchin."

"You do, dear Aunt Lois, if the rest of them do not, and you can tell me."

"That is a very good way," said the old lady, "and we have run on very happily on that principle. You know I am proud of you, and well I may be.

"But this will not do forever. There are some things to be gained among more people—some things which you will never get if you stay always tied to my apron.

"Rachel, how should you like to go to the Mount Kearsarge Seminary?"

"I should not like it at all," said Rachel bluntly, "and I do not think I had better go."

This was an unpromising beginning. But all the same to the Mount Kearsarge Seminary Rachel went. Her affectionate assurances that she was perfectly satisfied with the Hitchin High School went for nothing. A subtle plan to postpone the evil day for a year went for less. Aunt Lois had made up her mind that it was well for the girl to be flung upon the world on her own resources. She did not say so to Rachel, but this furnished her real motive for a separation which cost her a great deal.

"Bring me that book you were reading to me at Waterville," she said.

"Which book, Aunt Lois?"

"Why, Mr. What's-his-name's. You know — the book with a purple cover." This was an old joke between them, and the book appeared.

"There, Rachel, I thought of you when you were reading. For I had this on my mind all the time I was there. Changing the things which are to be changed, as Parson Caner says—here is the passage:

"I do not suppose that this is the best school in the world unless you make it so. But I do suppose you can make it so. If you and I went whining about, looking for the best school in the world, I should die, and you would lose your voice with whining, and we should not find one after all. This, as it happens, is what the public provides for us."

And so, with short shrift poor Rachel was swung off to what seemed to her almost like a small boat fleeing from shipwreck. But Aunt Lois broke the fall. She went part way with her. They went to Boston to make some last purchases, which both of them supposed to be necessary, and then on Monday morning Aunt Lois accompanied the girl to the Albany station and left her in the train for the Connecticut River.

It was more than three years since Rachel first landed in Boston, and in all that time no one of the passengers in the Baikal had ever been heard from, excepting those who landed with her on that summer morning. Of these John Wolff was the only one Rachel had ever seen. Captain Jucker had written a short letter, with some difficulty, in answer to a short letter also written with difficulty by Rachel. Aunt Lois had pronounced that a correspondence need not be maintained, to which neither party showed much inclination. "Fetich!" she said. John Wolff had obtained Rachel's address from Miss Child, and from his home in Iowa had written. The letter had been accompanied by a cordial note from his mother, confirming the invitation her son had given, that Rachel should visit them if she ever went to the West.

To this letter Aunt Lois dictated the answer.

This summer they had met John Wolff. He was trout-fishing in the White Mountains, and he made his home at Greeley's, where they were staying. Of course the sight of him brought back the old memories. But Rachel would not brood, and if she had wished to Aunt Lois would not let her. Indeed, from temper and from duty, she kept her hands so full that her heart was not apt to be sad. He had met her first on the hotel piazza. He turned suddenly and said, " Surely it is Miss Rachel Finley?"

"Surely it is," said Rachel, not wholly sadly, partly laughing indeed, though the sight of him had made her sad. "I ought to have spoken to you, and in a minute more I would; I was curious, though, to see if you would know me."

"You are very much changed. You are taller, and—"

If he had dared he would have said, "You are a woman now, and you were a girl then."

"Yes," said Rachel hastily, "I am very much changed. I am more changed than you are. For you are not changed at all, Mr. Wolff. I knew you in a moment, but I had no idea that you were here."

And by this time her aunt had moved her chair far enough on the seat to make room for him between them. He accepted the opportunity. Rachel presented him to her friends, and went on:

"You are the first—you are the only one—of—of—our sea-friends I have ever seen—or—" and this she said as bravely as she could, though the tears were streaming down her face—" or ever shall see—in this world."

"How strange it is!" he said. "How strange it is! How strange it all was! I would not give up for months. I did not give up for months. It would be fair to say that I do not give up now, Miss Finley."

"No," said Rachel sadly, "you must not say that to me. I have given up. It is better that I should. As our second rule says, I had better look forward to meeting them than to look back. I know that for this world all is over. But, of course, I never forget. I never go to bed at night but I think of that last night on the ship, or the night in the boat, and those strange nights in the kind skipper's stateroom."

And so the ice had been broken, and they talked for half an hour as if they had been together every day for these five years. She told him and he told her of the gradual fading out of hope. But in his case there had been no such personal agony as in hers. She told him, without detail, of Hitchin and her home there—that, in spite of herself and without meaning to, she had grown to be a New Hampshire girl. "You would not know me from the original, Mr. Wolff. I 'ride in a boat,' I could 'teach a school,' I have 'good times,' and I never say 'nice' or 'nasty.'"

As Rachel bade Mrs. Winchell good-by she certainly felt homesick, as she settled herself in the car and as the train passed out from the station. From this moment must begin the learning of new faces and new names, without one chance of meeting a person even as familiar as the driver of the omnibus. But there was nothing to cry for, and she did not cry. She made a vigorous effort to interest herself in the panorama which flew by, and then, when the steam from the engine cut her off from this indulgence, she began a systematic study of her fellow-passengers.

Cattle dealers returning from market had not much interest for her, nor "drummers" or commercial travellers, had she known enough of the business of the country even to guess who they were. But why were there so many young girls—girls of almost her own age?

Could there be a picnic to which they were all going? They had lunch-baskets—or similar provision—just as she had.

Was America the country of independent young women, as she knew she had heard her Aunt Ann say before she ever left home?

These girls seemed to know each other generally. But not always. Rachel noticed, with a certain sympathy, that one who sat quite alone in a corner had been crying, and that she did not fall in with the chatter of the others, who, on their part, had nothing to do with her.

If Rachel did not know America she did know how to travel, almost by instinct. Knocked about as she had been, with her own canoe to paddle, as an admirable national proverb says, she was not fated to starve to death on a railroad train because she had no courier or other servant to take care of her. Accordingly, when at half past eleven or thereabouts, the train stopped at the noisy, reckless, ill-ordered junction at Springfield, Rachel boldly made a foray from the car, asking a fussy conductor how much time she had, and worked her way by instinct to the refreshment-room. A party of waiters within an oval counter were doing their best to attend to an army of passengers, who should have met four times as many attendants. With that magic which compelled one of these girls, not unwilling, to obey her, Rachel produced her tin travelling flask provided for her by Mrs. Winchell's forethought, instructed the girl how to prepare her coffee and fill the flask, selected the form of biscuit which she fancied most, and retired in triumph to the train. As they resumed their journey the flask was made to provide a little tin cup from its own cover, and across the passage-way Rachel spoke to the lonely girl.

"Drink a little of my warm coffee. I had no sugar in it. Do you like sugar? There is some in this paper."

The other girl raised herself, smiled a little sadly, and refused the coffee at first, from that traditional New England habit which refuses everything one wants, from a feeling that virtue lies in abnegation. But Rachel was not rebuffed so easily.

"Indeed, you must drink some. There is more than both of us can drink. If you were as old a traveller as I, you would know that not to take food enough in travelling makes headache. And to take too much makes you stupid." She laughed, and the other laughed, then took off her glove, dropped a lump of sugar in the little mug, and drank it all.

"It is very nice, and I am sure I thank you. I have some lunch somewhere, but I had forgotten it."

So she produced the stores which that pale, pretty mother of hers had left with her, while Rachel opened Aunt Lois's basket. Then the girl who had a mother cleared the seat opposite her for the girl who had none, and asked her to cross the passage and join her. And it proved that both of them were hungry with the healthy appetites of seventeen, and that in the bustle of leaving home neither of them had eaten much breakfast. They tempted each other with the various delicacies of the two commissariats, and soon became at ease with one another.

And then it proved that Lina Whitman also was going to the Mount Kearsarge Seminary, and it proved, alas! that it was her first long absence from home.

It was clear enough to both of them that at Springfield the car had taken on many more girls, some of whom had been welcomed with rapture by those already on board. Now, therefore, they were quite sure that most if not all of this chattering, merry company of their fellow-travellers were to be companions for more than one half day; and in their new-born confidence in each other they began a series of quiet speculations as to the rest— how they should like the chip-hat girl, whether the black-eyed girl were cross or only pretended to be, and so on.

And thus they were quite at home with each other, and neither of the two felt lonely when the conductor called "Schairer's Crossings," and the whole host of young women rose, and gathered parasols, baskets, parcels of books, shawl-straps, and luncheon wrecks, and pressed forward and pressed backward out of the car, which they left nearly desolate. At the little station were six or eight omnibuses in waiting, and jovial drivers and conductors with whom the "old girls" seemed good-naturedly familiar. A tremendous debarkation of luggage took place. But for this the school-girls did not wait. They only gave their baggage-checks to the drivers of special wagons, and they themselves clambered with their wealth of hand-luggage into the omnibuses. As soon as a coach was filled the driver cracked his whip and was off, making great pretence of eagerness that his particular convoy should arrive early at the school. In fact it was a drive of four miles, over a pretty rolling country such as Rachel or Lina had never seen before. The roads were none too smooth and were quite too dusty, so that nobody was sorry when they reached the great castle built of wood around four sides of a square, in which these sixty girls, and four hundred others as good as they, were to live together with no assistance from the other sex for the next four months of their lives.

A great company of jolly, hearty young women of their own age met them all on the steps. Whether they were other students who had arrived before the travellers, or whether they were the servants of the school, did not appear at first. Eventually it proved that they were both. For, under the sensible discipline of this place, every girl who was there to study had to lend a hand in the necessary work of the establishment, and was detailed to duty from day to day, having to do now twenty minutes' work, now seventy minutes every day, according as the work assigned were accounted hard or easy. Some such familiar pounced on Lina and Rachel as they looked around them doubtfully, and with small ceremony hurried them up two flights of stairs, and through a long passage-way, till she came to an open door. She looked in, seemed satisfied, and said, "Yes, this will do for to-day. Come in and make yourselves comfortable. You two can stay here if you like till rooms and room-mates are assigned. That will be after examinations."

"Examinations!" cried both the new girls, aghast.

"Why, yes, don't you know? Examinations, you know, to see if you can stay. But, of course, you will stay. Everybody stays if she knows that twice one is two. I believe that really the examinations are for them to find out about room-mates, you know.

"Anyway, wash yourselves now and fix up. There are no studies to-day. And by and by you will hear the bell ring for supper, and then will be chapel. You'll find the other girls all waiting down-stairs."

And so she bade them good-by and left them. The

little room they were in was tidy, not uncomfortable, though a little bare. A bed big enough for both, with a mattress and two pillows in it, but without sheets and pillow-cases, was not inviting for repose. None the less did the two girls avail themselves of its welcome. They knew that when their trunks arrived, which would be in a few minutes, they would be expected to produce their own stores of linen for it. Two chairs and a table with shelves for books, on which lay two Bibles, and one looking-glass not dangerous to vanity, completed the furniture of this room. There opened from it a little room or large closet, lighted by ground glass from the larger room, and in this was a washstand and toilet furniture. The girls learned afterward that each girl was expected to spend most of one hour of every day quite alone for serious meditation or for devotion. The two rooms were arranged so that each might have such daily seclusion.

Teachers, pupils, and governesses of the seminary were all Protestants of the tenth power, or higher, if a higher power can be thought effective. But, if they had known it, they had contrived a school which reflected many of the conditions of a Catholic convent. As has been said, each girl of the five hundred had her own personal share of the duties of the household, and the theory was that before her course at the school was over, she would be trained in practice of each of the departments of housekeeping, even were that housekeeping as extensive as a duchess must carry on. By a very curious law, which had been wrought out in the natural selection of many years, these duties were balanced against each other on a scale founded on their ease or difficulty. Thus the daily term of the girl to attend the door-bell lasted several hours, because it was supposed to be easy, and indeed agreeable. A girl at the wash-tub would have a much shorter period of duty than a girl who was clear-starching, a term midway between these extremes. I am assured that in a convent a lady abbess would have doomed her nuns to one or another of these duties by a somewhat arbitrary decision. I am sure that in a phalanstery each girl would have done the duty she was attracted to do, but here at Kearsarge the rule was as unflinching as if John Calvin had made it himself, as indeed indirectly he had. That is to say, there was absolute equality before the law. One week Rachel was responsible for putting the tablecloths and napkins on the tables, one week she had the forks in charge, and one week the knives. One week she washed, and one week she ironed, and one week she was up earlier than the rest, that she might put the biscuits into the oven. Sometimes her work took her twenty minutes of the day, sometimes it kept her three times as long, but the short day's work was hard and the long day's work was easy. But the winepress, whatever it was, was never trodden alone; all work was lighter because it was done amid a troop of laughing girls, whose sires were far away at work in very different affairs.

As for the teaching from books and the learning from books, both were first-rate. Rachel did not at the time understand how curiously unlike the rest of the world the school was in the intensity of its purpose. But she learned afterward to look back with a certain wonder on the life they led there, wholly engrossed in their own concerns, and as indifferent to the affairs of the rest of the world as passengers in a ship in mid-ocean are to the affairs of the Sultan of Timbuctoo.

Outside the school there was a joke, which had come even to Rachel's ears, which implied that it was established for the purpose of educating wives for foreign missionaries, and memories of this joke occasionally lighted up the tables when some gray-haired doctor of divinity or other member of the board of trustees came to dine with the principal. On such occasions the merriest would pretend to be on their best behavior at table, as if to make sure that the longed-for choice of early martyrdom might fall upon them. But this was really nothing but a joke, and in practice the interest of the school was in algebra, arithmetic, geometry, Latin, or French, studied as if they were ultimate realities or entities in themselves, and with curiously little thought in either case what they were studied for.

But this little book must not concern itself with the interesting record of the methods of instruction pursued at Mount Kearsarge. For these the disappointed reader must turn to the catalogues of the day, and the files, yet in MS., of the annual reports of the hard-worked teachers to the omnipotent trustees. Our business is rather with Rachel Finley, and even of her life much of the detail must, alas! be passed over. We must choose—let us only hope we choose wisely—what may best illustrate her varied fortunes.

The school, although founded by the purest of Puritans, was not without certain relaxations, and the girls were not slow to push these to the very farthest. Wherever an inch was granted an ell was taken. Walks, and long walks, were within their range, with no need of escort in that simple and well-governed country region— well-governed because left to its own governance. As for riding, as the vernacular called what the English prefer to call driving—as to going in a carriage drawn by horses, in the manner in which the eunuch went when he "rode in his chariot"—the girls were limited more by their purses than by the rules of the school. When

Saturday came, with some exemption from school duty, any girl who chose might hire a horse and wagon from the Hobson of the place, and take any other girl on an excursion. For masculine escort there was little chance and little favor. A girl might go to ride with her father, or with her brother, or with the fortunate man to whom she was engaged, but with no other man.

Maria Kent, an audacious friend of Rachel's, once went to the principal to ask permission to go to ride with Mr. Wilcox.

"And who is Mr. Wilcox, Miss Maria?"

"He is a friend of mine, from Kentish Town."

"You know the rules, Miss Maria; he is certainly not your father."

"No," said Maria, demurely.

"You have no half-brother named Wilcox?"

"No," said poor Maria.

"Are you engaged to the gentleman?"

"No," said Maria, "but I shall be before we come home."

But the request, under this half and half submission, could not be gratified.

Rachel was in her second year in the school, when as the term drew near its close, the energetic girls, who were the self-constituted captains in such affairs, arranged a party to the top of the mountain. Any girl might go who had enough of her spending money left to contribute the moderate assessment, and, as it proved on this occasion, more than a hundred agreed to go. The good-natured drivers of the omnibuses and stages were consulted, and brought together from neighboring villages enormous covered vehicles used now to carry furniture, now men, women, and children, and which, in the more recent vernacular, are known as barges. In these great arks the young folks were to be carried five or six miles well up the lower slope of the mountain, and the last pull of the ascent, a hard walk of a mile or two more, was to be made on foot. Then, indeed, the real frolic of the expedition was to begin.

Half a dozen of the teachers went with them. Indeed, the day would have been regarded as imperfect had they declined. For there was generally little difference in age between scholars and teachers—there was almost none in purpose—for every teacher was a learner and owned it, and the whole convent was on the most cordial relations between rulers and ruled. The teachers and the more experienced girls became, of course, guides to the others, after the real climbing of the mountainside on foot began.

So it happened that Rachel with Lina and Miss Haverstock were in a group together, with their hands full of lady's-slippers which Lina had brought in in triumph from an excursion on one side, and all three were trying to make up for their lost time by cutting off a corner in an ascent steeper than the regular roadway took, when they came on a young man and young woman sitting alone, as if to rest ; if, indeed, they had not gone aside intentionally, to be the more free from observation.

The young woman was not one of the Kearsarge party. She was flushed, perhaps with walking. Her straw hat swung in her hand.

The three passed hastily by, almost affecting not to see the two, although it were hard not to tread on them. But they did not pass so quickly but that Rachel saw that the young man was John Wolff.

Yes, John Wolff of the Baikal and of the fishing schooner and Waterville.

Did John Wolff recognize her, Rachel wondered. But she did not know, nor did she much care.

"When can one be off one's guard?" cried Lina, laughing. "To think that we should have broken in on a scene so tender!"

"Oh no, not tender," said tolerant Miss Haverstock. "The girl had a toothache. He was probably the dentist from New Padua, and he was trying to make her have her tooth pulled."

"I wish I knew," said Lina. "But mean as I am I will leave them alone and will not play spoil-sport again."

And with walking, and straggling, and stopping for lady's-slippers, and Linnæa, and dwarf-cornel, and then with hurrying on to make up lost time, some alone, some lost and found again, some in jolly groups, the end of two hours found them on the top of the mountain. Three or four acres of wood had been cut off by sylvan lovers of the grander picturesque, that the prospect, almost infinite, might be enjoyed by people who did not climb trees. From a few of the logs a rough cabin had been built by way of celebrating the Fourth of July, by a band of jolly communists, who did not know that the very institution of society itself would be perilled, if men united together for the common good and were not paid for their labors. Into this cabin and to its simple luxuries such people retired as needed to refit themselves from any accident of travel. A closet in it provided two or three frying-pans and one or two tin cans which other communists had left for the general good. A scouting party was already at work bringing in water from great gulfs in the rocks, well known to earlier explorers. Every cloud that rested on the mountain left its tribute in these clefts, and clear water distilled into them for the benefit of bird, beast, and man. From such rocky cisterns was first of all collected the primal necessity for mankind and womankind tired and faint.

Strange to say, the scouting party bringing in the water to the communistic tubs and pails was not a party of Kearsarge students, nor of stout "daughters of the plough," sent in advance to prepare for them.

It was a party of young gentlemen, students of the University at New Padua, a college which was about six miles from the mountain on the north, as the girls' seminary was six miles away on the south.

The gentlemen made no expression of surprise at seeing the ladies, nor did the ladies on their side. Yet there was not, in fact, one girl of all of them who had really known that these young men would be there. Only there always was such a party there when the Kearsarge girls went up together. Somehow the young men found it out, and made their plans for an excursion on the same day. They went up on the north side and arrived a little earlier than the girls did. The leaders of the girls' party were never afraid that they should not find the pails and tubs and basins full of water, a good fire burning, and men enough to refill the little tanks when they were empty.

"Miss Dudley," said Maria Kent, "will you let me present to you my friend, Mr. Wilcox? You have heard me speak of him. He is one of our Kentish Town boys —the one you thought was my half-brother," said the bold girl, as a final shot of triumph.

And it may be hoped that before that day was over Mr. Wilcox had earned the right to take Maria Kent on a drive whenever there was a half holiday at the Mount Kearsarge Seminary.

Here, then, was the mystery accounted for—if it had

seemed a mystery to Rachel—of Mr. John Wolff's appearance.

It was not long before he joined her, this time without the blushing or flushed young girl. Was she blushing, or was she only flushed with climbing? Mr. Wolff hovered round Rachel and Lina and Miss Haverstock as they sat on a heavy bed of hemlock, and as he and the other gentlemen brought coffee and sandwiches and other stores from the picnic provided. So soon as she recognized him he joined their party, and was on good terms at once with all.

In the midst of young folks' chatter and joke, "And now," he said, repeating the perfectly hackneyed joke, "you are to go out as a missionary, I suppose."

"Oh, that is as Aunt Lois says. She is a despot, a very kind despot, and she does with me just what she will."

As it happened Rachel often thought of this joking speech afterward. For the moment he was called away by one of the masters of the revels, who wanted him to help in carrying off and washing a great coffee-kettle. He said he should be back in a moment. But before he returned Miss Harlan, one of the second assistants, came to Rachel and Lina, thinking that they needed some guide, and asked them to come and see the smoke from her father's house on the other side of the valley. Had Rachel told the whole truth she would have said, "I should rather not see the smoke. I should rather stay and talk with Mr. Wolff." But, under such circumstances, people generally keep back some part of the truth. At all events, Rachel did. She went with Miss Harlan to the other side of the hill-top. And when John Wolff came back to the throne of hemlock boughs none of the princesses whom he had left were there.

As it happened, too, he mistook the directions which Drum, a sophomore whom he found there, gave him for following them. He lost himself in a heavy thicket of laurel, and what it is to do that no one but he who feels it knows. It was with his clothes torn and his hands bleeding that he reappeared on the scene of action. It cost him a few minutes to repair and refit, that his aspect might be even decent for approach to ladies. When those few moments were over, the heads of the seminary party were counselling as to the best course to be taken in view of a black thunder-cloud which was rolling up in the south-west, and, as the weatherwise said, would take the mountain in its way before ten minutes were over.

Wisely or not the chiefs determined on immediate retreat to the barges, and such a retreat was ordered. Baskets, bags, shawls, and other hand-luggage were found or not found, as the case might be. The gentlemen from New Padua generally joined the seminary girls, to be of use in "carrying their traps" for them. But some of them had ladies of their own to care for. Among these was John Wolff. At the last moment, almost before the hurried flight began, he found Rachel and Lina.

"I was so sorry to miss you. I tore my face to pieces in that bramble bush where they said you had gone."

"Here is Miss Fiske, who came with me from New Padua; I wanted to introduce her to you."

"I am very glad to know you," said Rachel to the pretty girl, who was the same whom they had passed before in pretended unconsciousness, when she was flushed or blushing. "Will you not ride over and see us some day at the seminary?"

But whether she would or not Miss Fiske never told, for at that moment the first big drops from the sky fell.

One cry of laughter and surprise overpowered all other conversation, and the rear guard of the party was compelled by its chiefs, at a lively run, to follow the others down the rocky and tangled way.

If any one cares to know, every girl of the hundred pleasure-seekers was soaked to her skin, as she had never been soaked before, when they arrived at the barges.

They had sought pleasure, and for once they had found it. They agreed unanimously, as they rode home, that it was excellent fun.

Nor was one of the jolly party of omnipotents in the least the worse for the enterprise the next morning.

Such triumphs wait on the recklessness and vigor of seventeen.

CHAPTER VIII.

IS IT POSSIBLE?

"Fear no more the lightning flash
Nor the all-dreaded thunder storm."
Cymbeline.

As Rachel ran down-stairs the next morning she was intercepted by Mary Flanders, who was acting that month as a sort of page or errand girl to the head of the school.

"Miss Finley, Miss Dudley would like to see you."

"What—now? Who has the biscuits? How can I leave them?"

"Ellen Vose has been taken off the door and takes the biscuits, and Jane Flint is taken off the brass cleaning for to-day and takes the door. Anyway, Miss Dudley wants to see you now."

What could Miss Dudley want of her? The biscuits had been perfect all the month.

Not to chide her, certainly. Miss Dudley was not demonstrative in general. But on this occasion she rose from her chair the moment Rachel entered, fairly sprang toward her and folded her in her arms, and kissed her.

"My poor, dear Miss Rachel, I have bad news for you."

"Bad news for me, Miss Dudley?"

"Yes, my child. Perhaps you saw I was keeping something back last night. The telegram had just come. Your dear aunt, my dear friend, Mrs. Winchell—"

"Is sick?"

"Is dead!"

"My dear, dear Aunt Lois, my dear Aunt Lois! Is it possible?

"Miss Dudley, the dearest, kindest, sweetest, wisest friend a poor lost orphan ever had. My poor dear Aunt Lois!"

Miss Dudley led Rachel with her to her chair, sat down and let the girl rest in her arms, sobbing upon her neck.

Then she roused again. "How is it all? Tell me all you know. Why, I had a letter only yesterday! It is here now, and she says she is feeling particularly well! See here," said the girl, fumbling with the letter, in that determination, heaven-born and heaven-fostered, in which man or woman always refuses to believe death possible.

"Yes, dear, she must have been spared all suffering. They have made the despatch long to tell you that. Here it is:

"'Tell Miss Finley Mrs. Winchell suddenly killed by lightning. She died instantly. Letter by morning mail.—HANNAH VALENTINE.'

"Who is Hannah Valentine?" asked Miss Dudley.

"She is the head of the High School now. Aunt Lois is very fond of her, and she made our house her home this summer. She must have been in danger too. Killed by lightning! Why, Miss Dudley, it was our storm, the storm we laughed at so."

There was a strange feeling of neighborhood which came over Rachel as she spoke, as if she were glad that anything had united her to the danger of her dear friend.

And then Rachel was made to go into Miss Dudley's own parlor and lie on the sofa, and Lina, and Maria, and Cornelia, and all her nearest friends, vied with each other in thinking of little coddling and comforting things they could do for her. "I am not sick," said poor Rachel, once or twice, but she was all dazed and stunned ; and, indeed, the affection of the girls, no matter how it showed itself, was the only cordial which even the good God in heaven could administer to her at this moment. By and by faith and hope might come in with their special lessons. But now love must do the whole, as, in the hierarchy of duty and of life, often happens.

"You are so kind," said Rachel, as without a word that rattling Maria brought in six great lady's-slippers in a vase which she had borrowed from Miss Haverstock, and placed them where Rachel would see them, if she opened her eyes.

"You are so kind," said Rachel.

"Kind!" cried the impulsive girl, and she stooped and kissed her. "You know I would walk barefoot to Hartford to bring you a pin if the pin would only show you that I loved you." And what she said was true.

And at last the morning ground away, and the mail came up from the village. Here is the letter they had been waiting for :

Hannah Valentine to Rachel Finley.

" HITCHIN, Wednesday evening, June 3.

" MY DEAR, DEAR RACHEL : It is as sudden to us as it is to you. She had just rung the bell for tea. I was in my room, and heard the bell, and had my hand on the handle of my door, when the flash came. I was blinded.

I think I staggered, but in a moment all seemed clear, and I ran down to tell her that I thought I must have felt the shock.

"Rachel, she was lying on the floor of the hall. She was dead!

"We think that after she rang the tea-bell she walked forward to see the pile of clouds. I had been watching them from my window. You know she never was afraid of lightning. Strange to say, this was the first bolt, and I think the last. But, indeed, there might have been forty and I should not have known. I was working over her in every way I knew, but there was not a breath, not a sigh from the first. The doctor was here as soon as he could be, and Mr. Tyndale and the McClearys, and everybody has been so kind; but, oh, dear me, it is all dreadful!

"Come as soon as you can. I am lost without you.

"John McCleary is going to Boston on the night express and will mail this there. James took a telegraph for me before seven to Miss Dudley.

"My dear child, I am always your own
"HANNAH."

"You will hardly come back before the exhibition," said Miss Dudley, as Rachel bade her good-by when the coach was announced.

"Hardly," said Rachel. "You know we strained a point terribly with her before she would let me stay so long. 'Six months is enough, my dear,' those were her last words to me. And if you had not given me those six weeks at Christmas I should not be here now.

"It is of no use wishing I had been there. You know Dr. Withers told us we must never say 'if,' and I try not to think it."

And so with floods of tears Rachel bade her teachers and her other friends good-by. She did not know but she might return in October. But she knew nothing of the future. In point of fact, she never saw the seminary again.

No. As her fortunes opened before her, it proved that when Rachel's trunk was put upon the coach for the station, and when she entered it, she cut herself off from her old life as truly as when she fell into the sea and was hauled into the boat by John Wolff's strong arm.

Aunt Lois Winchell must have meant to make some provision for Rachel Finley in her will, but will, if she made one, was not found, has not been found to this hour. There followed a complete break-up, such as can hardly follow in this world, so complete in every detail, as in a village from which in fifty years every living being has emigrated, who was not anchored to it by what the law calls real property.

The colonel was long since dead. His room in the house, his portrait, and his sash, were all that remained to preserve his memory. Aunt Lois's sister had long since made her winter home in Florence and her summer home in the Tyrol. She was the heir-at-law. Of course the law knew nothing of such ties as bound Rachel to Aunt Lois. Strictly speaking, there was no more reason why she should spend an hour in that house than why she should stay in any other house in Hitchin.

There was the funeral. There was packing of Miss Lois's valuables, and making inventories of them, and of the books, to be sent to her sister. Mr. Tyndale and Mr. Barnard were appointed administrators, and then there was waiting to know what the wishes of Mrs.

Conolly were, as soon as a letter could be sent to Innspruck and a reply received. For she was travelling to and fro, and hurry was quite impossible. For a little, Rachel stayed in her old room, but after a little they shut up the dear old house. Nahum went his way, and the old servant-mistresses, who had long presided over different departments, went theirs. Rachel met Mr. Tyndale there, once and again, when he could make use of her. She took, as they bade her, and as in the end Mrs. Conolly bade her, some such little mementoes of her aunt as were of no cost in an appraisement. Mr. Tyndale went so far as to suggest to Mrs. Conolly that she should make to Rachel a present, and even named two or three thousand dollars as a proper sum. But Mrs. Conolly did not see the matter in that light. Because her sister had given a pleasant home to a young girl for three years, and had educated her at a good school for two more, she saw no reason why the family should continue to take care of her.

Such was the answer which Mr. Tyndale would have shown to Rachel with some indignation, had Rachel remained in Hitchin till it came. But Rachel was no longer there.

She had had no share in sending any message to Mrs. Conolly. She had never known Mrs. Conolly, nor had Mrs. Conolly ever known her. Rachel knew very well who was to take care of her.

It was Rachel Finley. And at the first she was embarrassed by the multitude of her advisers.

Mrs. Barnard at the other village drove over in some state, to ask her to come and spend a month with her till the affairs should all be settled, and the Conollys could be heard from. Indeed, there was a sheaf of invitations from different people in Hitchin. The most part of

Hitchin thought that one's first duty in life was to avoid leaving that town by any accident.

Miss Dudley sent a cordial invitation from the seminary. A few of the teachers were going to take their summer outing by staying there. Would not Rachel join their little home party?

But the invitation Rachel accepted was from Cecilia Vaughan.

Cecilia Vaughan to Rachel Finley.

"KEARSARGE SEMINARY, June 30.

"MY DEAR RACHEL: I have your second letter, and I am glad to see you are not quite a goose. I have written to my mother, and it is all settled.

"We must go alone, but that is no matter. It is one car all the way to Chicago.

"We shall be in Chicago from eight in the morning till three, then my uncle will take us to Lake Constance; and that evening, joy, joy, joy, you will see my father and my mother, and they will see you! I shall be perfectly happy! My father would come and meet us at Chicago, but that Uncle Jo is just as well.

"You are to stay all the summer till we go back to New Altoona. They opened the house at Lake Constance last Wednesday. There seem to have been thieves living in it at some part of the winter, but they have stolen nothing but a ducking gun, the second volume of 'Charles Grandison,' and a German dictionary. Those are thieves of some decency, are not they?

"Nobody but an English girl would have made me telegraph to my mother to know if she wanted you, as if I did not know! What's mine is hers and what's hers is mine.

"Meet me at Springfield, in the howling wilderness, when the 1 P.M. trains come together.

"Darling, I am always,

"CECILIA VAUGHAN."

CHAPTER IX.

FORGOTTEN TREASURE.

"*Sylvia.* Nay, take them.
Valentine. Madam, they are for you."
Two Gentlemen of Verona.

It was in the packing of her books, clothes, and other accumulations of five years, the destroying of letters, the giving away of keepsakes and other such cares which make the last days of any long residence hateful, and make any change tolerable, even were it to a ship's cabin, that Rachel came upon a waif long since wholly forgotten.

It was the share in the New England Stocking Company which Mr. Poore had given to her, at her first party.

"What is that elegant evidence of value, my dear child?" said Hannah Valentine. "I did not know that you were a 'bloated bondholder.'"

"Nor I," said Rachel, laughing. "I have not thought of this thing for years. I should have told you five minutes ago that my 'convertible assets,' as Mr. Barnard says, were forty-seven dollars, now in my pocket-book, and eleven cents, now in my purse.

"But, behold, I also am the owner of share No. 993 in the New England Stocking-Loom Company, value minus one cent. Hannah, I want to give you something. I will give you this, and you shall cut out the pictures for your hospital scrap-book."

"Are you sure it is worth nothing at all?" asked Hannah, less carelessly.

"I know that Mrs. Winchell thought it was nothing five years ago, and I believe that nothing at compound interest for five years generally amounts to nothing or less, when you are talking of business. But if you will not take it, why I remember Miss Willard would not take it at the Sewing Circle."

And she told Hannah the story. But, all the same, Hannah made her put by the envelope carefully. In the course of an hour Mr. Tyndale came in, and Hannah told him about the certificate.

"Worth anything? I should think so!" he said, laughing. "That pretty village you pass on the Boston and Maine, beyond William's Crossing, has grown out of the Stocking Loom. The last sale I heard of of the stock was when John Coram died. The shares were worth four or five hundred dollars then."

"Four or five hundred dollars! This scrap of paper worth four or five hundred dollars?"

"You say you have never drawn any interest? They divide sixty or eighty per cent a year. The shares were issued at fifty dollars, then they were a drug on the market. Afterward somebody else bought up what he could get. I congratulate you, Rachel. This is worth six or seven hundred dollars!"

"Then I shall read the story of Aladdin with more respect, Mr. Tyndale."

"And perhaps you will never give away any old lamps or old pamphlets. If I have taught you that I have taught you something," said he. "You had better write and ask who the officers are now, or I will write for you. Here is the address, 99 North Devonshire Street, Boston."

Rachel thanked him, and he went away. She put on her hat and went to the post-office, and asked to what place Mr. Poore had removed. She knew he no longer had any country home in Hitchin, as he had five years before, but there was no difficulty about his address. He was a partner in a great New York firm which received many packing-cases from Hitchin every week.

Rachel came home and wrote the following letter:

Rachel Finley to Thomas Poore.

"Hitchin, July 3.

"My dear Sir: You will find enclosed a paper which you placed in my hands in joke many years ago.

"I am mortified to find it to-day, and I beg you will understand that I had wholly forgotten it.

"Indeed, when I found it I should have destroyed it as being of no value, but that a friend tells me that it is really of very large value.

"Pray do not think that I have intentionally kept a valuable document, for, indeed, I had forgotten I had it; not to say that I believe I have never heard of the Stocking Company from that day to this.

"Respectfully yours,
"Rachel Finley."

"I cannot think you will remember me. I was a little girl, sitting by Miss Willard and Miss Cordis, when you were joking about the stockings."

Tom Poore, as all men called him, was taking the luxury of a holiday in his own private den high up toward heaven. He was above most men in New York, and a cool air drew through his windows. His day's work was done when somebody, who had a message from the warerooms below, came up the elevator and brought the " personal " mail.

" Hitchin" on the postmark struck Tom's eye, and he cut open the envelope. The other letters he left, for he was reading a novel by Cherbuliez, and had not meant to touch any letter. But he was fond of Hitchin.

Tom liked this letter. Nor was the subject a new one to him. He had gone backward and forward through its phases with Miss Ruth Cordis. Indeed, having his eyes open, he had, not long after he gave these two shares to the girls, invested a thousand dollars in the Stocking-Loom Companies of different districts, the New England Company among the rest. Taking them one with another, these stocks now represented to Tom a capital of about $250,000, the New England Company being by far the most valuable of all. Tom laid down the Cherbuliez, and wrote, on his most elegant paper, this note:

Thomas Poore to Rachel Finley.

" 943 DOANE STREET, NEW YORK, July 4.

" MY DEAR MISS FINLEY: You think my memory much worse than it is. I remember with great pleasure the evening we spent together at Mrs. Barnard's.

" You will find enclosed your share in the New England Stocking Company. I send this by registered mail, and you will have to give a receipt for it at your post-office.

" The share is in every sense yours. There is no method of book-keeping by which it could ever appear on my books as mine, unless, indeed, you will let me send you six hundred and seventy-one dollars and thirty-nine cents ($671.39), which is its value (at the rate of the last sales), with accrued interest, to-day.

"I shall gladly make this purchase if you wish, as it is for the interest of my firm to purchase as many outlying shares in small amounts as we can.

"Hoping often to meet you in our dear, dreamy Hitchin, I am very truly, your obliged servant,

"Thomas Poore."

This letter came to Hitchin as Rachel was waiting for the carriage which took her to the train. So she had to carry the certificate with her to Lake Constance. Once there she wrote the following letter at once:

Rachel Finley to Thomas Poore.

"Lake Constance, July 8.

"My dear Mr. Poore: As you will see from the enclosed, I received at Hitchin your kind letter and its enclosure.

"You have seen how unused to business I am, in my carelessness in enclosing to you anything so valuable in a letter not registered.

"I will not make such a mistake again.

"If it is hard to explain the transaction on your books, you will see it is impossible to explain it on mine.

"You paid something for the stock, and your books will show something for something.

"I have paid nothing for it, and therefore is it that I find no account to which I can charge it.

"Believe me, my dear sir, very respectfully yours,

"Rachel Finley."

When Rachel read this letter over she thought it a little hard or wooden as she said. Cecilia thought it very hard when she was consulted. But Rachel said that in such things the first essay was apt to be best. However, she consented to add this P. S.:

"I hope you do not think that I am acting as foolishly and rudely as I thought the treasurer of the society acted when you offered the shares to her. Believe me, I am very grateful for your kindness, and do not mean to be rude."

Tom Poore liked this letter as he had liked the other. The subject, as has been said, was not new to him, and he at once wrote this reply, which closed the correspondence :

Thomas Poore to Rachel Finley.

"Doane Street, New York City, July 11.

"My dear Miss Finley: I have your prompt and thoughtful note with the long-travelling certificate, and for both I am greatly indebted.

"I beg you to understand that I respect your scruples entirely, and am flattered that you are willing to express them to me.

"Will you pardon me if I say that I came, long since, to an amicable arrangement with Miss Cordis, who, as you may remember, received the third of these shares which seek a resting-place so vainly. She had difficulties not unlike yours, and mine were precisely the same as they are now.

"We agreed, finally, that on the 1st of January, 1900, we will all three meet at Tiffany's in New York.

"Miss Cordis reminded me that at Mrs. Barnard's house there was some such agreement.

"We are then to take ices together at Taylor's, and while we do so to tell how much good and how much harm the shares have done to us, to what uses we have devoted the proceeds, and what we will then do with what is left of them. Miss Cordis, in her bright way, has stated this in a contract which I have the honor to enclose. If it pleases you, I am sure she will be glad to consider you as a third party to the agreement.

"I have the honor to be, madam, with great respect, your obedient servant,

"THOMAS POORE."

After this Rachel thought she must go no further. She would take the stock for better for worse as a loan made to her by her good angel till the 1st of January, 1900, if that day ever came.

Rachel was not an Adventist, but she certainly had no "realizing sense" that she should be in the flesh when that date came round—nay, that it would come round.

And Tom Poore, who had been pleased with her whole bearing, handwriting, folding of her paper, and all, wrote this note to his niece Huldah Furness in Hitchin:

Thomas Poore to Huldah Furness.

"July 11.

"MY DEAR HULDAH: You must know some one who knows Miss Rachel Finley, who has lately left Hitchin. A friend of mine who knows her a little wants to see her photograph. Can you not get it for me? Do not make any fuss about it nor let any one know that you send it to me.

"Have you seen the new *Scribner?* I send a copy by this mail.

"Your affectionate uncle,

"TOM."

Huldah Furness to Thomas Poore.

"Hitchin, July 13.

"My dear Uncle: This is an easier commission than you sent me about the mushrooms. Rachel Finley—well, she is my *dearest friend*, and the nicest girl in this world. I wish it was you that wanted to know how pretty she is and not some rubbishy friend of yours. I suppose it is about her lost father and mother, but I am not even curious about them, for I know they will never be found. Here is the picture. Is not she just lovely? You must send it right back, for she gave it to me herself, and I cannot live without it.

"Thank you for the *Scribner*, and thank you always for being so nice and good.

"Your own little

"Huldah."

Tom Poore did think the picture was "just lovely." He took it at once to a photographer, ordered a copy of it of twice the size of the card to be made on porcelain, and in three days Huldah had her card again.

Tom's porcelain, framed in velvet, hung by the side of the window in his sleeping-room. Tom went himself to a shop where he was not known and bought a small gold ring.

CHAPTER X.

LAKE CONSTANCE.

"And when at eve his fellow pilgrims sat,
Discoursing of the Lake,—asked where it was."
Samuel Rogers.

WE have gone a little before our story in introducing Rachel's letter from Lake Constance, but it seemed more convenient to put those business matters out of the way.

It should be explained to dull readers that this Lake Constance is not in Switzerland. Who shall say indeed that this ungeographical writer has not mistaken the name? Yet those letters can scarcely be wrong. Probably within fifty years it was known as Burned Slab Pond, or Gosham's Lake, or by some other detestable name. Constance we will call it now.

Life at Lake Constance was, as it proved, just the best change and the best tonic for poor Rachel. Excepting her friend Cecilia there was no one in all the company at that gay watering-place whom she had ever seen before. And although one may call it a gay watering-place, life can be as tranquil in such a house as Mr. Vaughan's, as ever a lady abbess might choose to order, if there were a lady abbess there. In the mere externals everything was different from what it was at Kearsarge or Hitchin. There the sun rose and set behind mountains, here everything was level. There the forests were mostly evergreen, here every tree was of what the natives would have called "hard wood." More than this, in these centres of civilization at the East, every one from early morning to late evening had a duty on hand or apologized for not having one. But in this summer holiday at the West, no one pretended to have any all day long.

Life passed easily enough in long sessions at table, in reading aloud, in bathing, rowing, and sailing, in walking, riding on horseback, or driving, in long siestas, in charade parties, and in card parties. In the jolly circle at the great hotel a set of irrepressible young people got up hops, and concerts, and theatricals, and occasionally celebrated a holiday by an evening display of fireworks and by bringing together in such festivities every tug and boat upon the lake with weird displays of many-colored lanterns. The people in the cottages, to which superior class the Vaughans and Rachel for the moment belonged, did or did not take part in these amusements. They could join in them if they chose; they need not join if they did not choose.

Some very energetic people kept up a book club, and so you had more novels than you knew what to do with, and more magazines than you ever heard of, all on the virtual condition that you should read none of them. Once a week the book club met at one house or another for afternoon tea, and you heard a paper read on the correlation of forces, or on the color of the eyelashes of Thalaba, according as the man or woman of letters, who was the light of the afternoon, happened to have studied the one subject or the other.

Thus tranquilly passed ten weeks of this happy corner of Elysium. Then the Arabs who lived in it folded their tents and went back to the clamor and clangor of autumn, of winter, and of spring. Hotels and cottages were left alone to the tender mercies of dying flies and of tramps, until another June brought in the housemaid, the painter, the glazier, and the purveyor, to make all ready for another summer.

Poor Rachel needed some time to come to her bearings. Her friends knew how terrible had been the strain and pressure upon her, and prudently left her much alone. For herself, she discovered the resources of her new home for rest, refreshment, and life, and gradually she tested them.

The girl was a fearless oarsman, as she had been used to boats both at Hitchin and at Kearsarge. She caught readily from Tom Vaughan the notion of the curved stroke of the paddle of the canoe, and afterward gladly took his permission to use his birch for lonely cruises. She learned very soon which of the pretty coves of Lake Constance is shady in the morning and which in the afternoon. With the pretence of reading, and sometimes the reality, she took possession of one or another every morning, and if no party to ride or drive or sail formed itself in the afternoon she was apt to take her canoe alone then.

It was a little late on one of the August afternoons which she had thus spent by herself, when, as she returned, she passed a gentleman in one of the smaller boats; sailing with such little wind as offered. He touched his hat, as, in the simple courtesies of Lake Constance, every gentleman on the water did to every lady. Rachel, like all people who paddle, was facing in the direction in which the canoe was going, and she did not observe that the boatman at once tacked and ran into the little landing-place. For herself she loitered on the way home, and when she reached the shore he came to the landing plank to meet her. She did not know him, but she was not surprised that he held the canoe till she had landed, nor that he fastened it fore and aft to the stakes where it belonged. Such an attention from a gentleman to a lady was by no means obtrusive in the cordial life of Lake Constance.

But when this was done and Rachel had thanked him, he touched his hat again, and said, "I think I am speaking to Miss Finley."

"Yes," said she, " but I am ashamed to say that I do not recognize you."

"There is no reason why you should be ashamed. We have not met for many years, indeed we hardly met then, though we have had some correspondence. I am Mr. Thomas Poore."

Rachel laughed and welcomed him cordially to Lake Constance. Who was he visiting? It proved that he was at the hotel. He had heard that she was at Mr. Vaughan's, and had taken the liberty to call. But not finding her, he had been tempted to try one of the boats, which he had found neat and easily handled.

Of course they walked to the house together, and at Rachel's invitation he came in. As it happened, a dozen other people had dropped in, by one accident or invitation or another, and the piazza tea party was larger than usual. After tea the children got up some charades in the back parlor. The visitors generally took an interest and eventually took part. And so, before the evening was over, Mr. Thomas Poore, who was by no means shy or ignorant of the way to live and to talk, was on sufficiently good terms with all the company. He walked home with those who came from his hotel, six or eight persons as it happened. Before lunch the next morning they had made him feel at ease with a dozen or twenty others. And so, nobody ever guessed that when Mr. Poore had taken his solitary dinner in that house on the day of his arrival, he knew no human being at Lake Constance by sight, or by name, except Miss Rachel Finley. That she was there he had learned from the date of her letter written some weeks before. How Miss Rachel herself looked, he had learned from her porcelain counterfeit in his own private room. That Lake Constance proved to be the pleasant, easy, lazy, lively place that it is, was luck much better than Mr. Poore had for a moment hoped for, when he determined to give himself his August holiday in that part of the country. That Mr. Vaughan's summer house should prove to be about as pleasant a house for July and August as there is in the world, was certainly much more than he had expected. He had taken his chances, and he had found that fortune favors the brave.

"Mrs. Vaughan," said Mr. Poore, one pleasant morning, when he surprised them all at breakfast, "we have at our house a very learned antiquary, who is here studying the portrait mounds, those queer things which look like buffaloes, or horses, or dogs, or men, if you make believe very hard. We have been making a party to go with him this afternoon to see the bear and eagle on the Pottawatomie Divide, and perhaps we shall find that it is the lion and the unicorn. I hoped we might find some recruits here. My carriage will hold three or four more : can I not tempt any of you ?"

Mrs. Vaughan was gracious and good-natured. Her husband pooh-poohed the whole thing. He had owned three buffaloes and two brooms, he believed ; the buffaloes were five hundred feet long, and each broom was as long as three buffaloes. "I kept them, from reverence to antiquity, for five years," said he, "but I found they were much more easily studied in the pictures than in fact, and I told Cephas last summer that he might plough over the buffaloes, which was a great comfort to him."

But Cecilia was not to be laughed out of a pleasant afternoon excursion so easily ; and after an early lunch, Mr. Poore, triumphant as always, came round in a handsome open barouche. Tom Vaughan mounted the seat with the driver ; Mrs. Vaughan, Cecilia, and Rachel made the party within.

And a very jolly party they were.

Arrived at the eagle and the unicorn, as Cecilia insisted on calling the antiquities, the party broke up into groups, trios, and couples, as had been foreordained. Cecilia found friends among the McKenzies, Mrs. Vaughan was tired with her ride and established herself under her umbrella, just where the eagle's beak sheltered her from the wind, and Mr. Poore took Rachel down the ravine to show her the vista down the lake and the distant prairie.

"Mrs. Vaughan is a pleasant person," said he, "and their house is charming. I do not remember them at Hitchin."

"Oh, no, they are not New Hampshire people. I met Cecilia at school."

"You are here for the summer ?"

"Yes," said she, "Cecilia and I have been inseparable at school, and we could not bear to give it up even when we came to an end."

"I remember just that feeling," said he. "At my class-supper—that means the end, you know—we stood together in the college campus to see the sun rise ; we shook hands and said ' good-by ;' and, Miss Finley, of the twenty men I know best, I have not seen five from that day to this."

"And men have better chances to travel than women."

"Had. Yes, perhaps they have. Only when a young man travels he travels with a hat full of duties. He must see this man, he must consult that firm. His employers will not like to find that he staid two days in Arcadia because Jim Johnson had married his pretty wife there."

Rachel laughed. "But then the man can leave the train and take the next. He can just shake hands with Jim Johnson and make up his employer's time by riding all night. Women are much more tied to the programme."

"I have thought of that. It must be a bore to have your route and all planned out for you; to have the man come in and say, 'We shall take the nine forty,' so grandly, without even telling you why."

"Cecilia and I wanted very much to stay over a train in Rochester. But the things were checked through, and of course we must follow our baggage."

"As when you read history it says, 'He was encumbered by his baggage train.' What would these buffalo and eagle makers say to us tramps desecrating their sacred shrines?"

"Have you the slightest faith in the shrines?" asked Rachel, who, like him, had heard the professor's lecture.

Mr. Poore laughed and made a mock gesture of terror. "We should not be permitted to ride home with them if we talked treason. It all looks very well on the map. I guess it is all right."

"Any way," said she, "we will fight for our antiquities to the last drop of our blood. You should have heard me defend the Gothic architecture of Chicago last week."

"The Gothic architecture of Chicago! Who attacked it?"

"Oh, a grand English lady whom we had here. Her husband is professor of applied bad manners in Oxford, I believe. She said that there were churches in Chicago where two parts were fifty years different from each other."

"What did you tell her?"

"I wanted to tell her that she should have staid at home."

"But, Miss Finley, are not you an English girl?"

"All the more have I a right to take down my countrywomen. Yes, I am an English girl, but I believe that makes me a more terrible Yankee."

"You are not so very terrible," said he.

"Take care, Mr. Poore, you do not know me. Now tell me about Ruth Cordis. Where is she? She did not stay long in Hitchin. Alas! nobody does."

"You know what Mr. Webster said of New Hampshire, that it was a good place to move from."

"Shame on him! How gladly would I have spent my life in Hitchin."

"With an occasional paddle in Lake Constance?"

And so they chattered on, the girl perfectly unconscious of his deep-seated purpose, he perfectly willing to enjoy the hour and to bide his time. Why there were not forty rivals eager to part him from this lovely girl, whom he believed to be a noble woman, he could not conceive. As, by good fortune, there were none, he could enjoy his afternoon, and he need not give her an instant's alarm, and might work his way along to that easy familiarity of intercourse in which all things are possible.

Happy Thomas Poore!

Unconscious Rachel Finley!

The expedition returned with perfect success. What

was the report at the hotel need not here be told, but as the cottage party all sat late over one of Mrs. Vaughan's luxurious teas, they agreed unanimously that never had anybody planned anything which had come off more perfectly.

And so Tom Poore won his spurs in the little company at Lake Constance, and was recognized as being by divine right one of the honorable self-appointed company of those who suggest and carry out the amusements of mankind. He was well fitted for this service. He was handsome, good-tempered, and rich. He had good executive capacity and did not care to be praised. He was perfectly willing to make a plan, and then to have somebody else take all the credit of it, or, for that matter, to have forty people do so. At the present moment he had one very distinct purpose in his own mind. He wanted, before winter, to make use of the little gold ring which lay hidden in the inner pocket of his portemonnaie. But he knew that this charming woman did not like him as much as he liked her. Nay, he was no fool, and he knew there was no reason why she should. He had made his plan—made it too carefully perhaps. For this was not a matter of the buying of a factory or of the controlling of a market. But none the less Tom had made it. And as he thought it was a good plan he meant to carry it through. Certainly at Lake Constance fortune still favored the brave.

Before long he had announced in the hotel to some one of his familiars, that instead of a week he meant to spend the rest of the summer at Constance, and he had had his traps moved down into a corner room. Then his mail began to come. It was just the least bit odd to be the mail of a business man. It had the queerest number of English and French journals; as it happened it had one or two which Miss Vaughan or Rachel had expressed a curiosity about. Tom had boldly said that they were sent regularly to him and that he would order them from New York. Regularly sent they were in a sense, for such things are regularly sent from Europe for any one who wants them in America. Tom, in this instance, was the man who wanted them. And when the *Rundschau* appeared at Rachel's breakfast two days after she had alluded to it, it never occurred to her that the order for it danced over the wire to New York, before she was asleep, on the night when they were all talking on the piazza. In many such ways Tom Poore found it in his power to be of use to the little company at Lake Constance.

Mrs. Vaughan took to him almost from the beginning. He was just what her establishment needed, in the hierarchies of the social order of the place. For her husband was far too lazy to keep the run of what was going on, and Tom was too young. Tom cared for nothing but riding his pony, and fishing, and an occasional baseball match. But with Mr. Poore she was quite safe. And now, if the Emperor of Brazil should come to spend a couple of days with Mrs. Harris, why the Vaughans would be able to do the right thing; they would not let him come and go without any notice, as they did the Queen of Honolulu. In that case the Queen had proved to be a humbug, as Mr. Vaughan always reminded his wife. But she might have been genuine. And Mrs. Vaughan was far too sincere in her hospitality, to be willing to have even the Emperor of Brazil escape her.

For poor tired Rachel, shocked through and through, more than her English nature wholly showed, by the calamity which had robbed her of a mother for a second time, the Constance life was the best tonic that could have been devised.

"My dear child," said Mrs. Vaughan, "you are to forget that you have a duty."

"Oh, indeed, Mrs. Vaughan, that will be hard. You could let me sit on a cushion if you had a seam you wanted me to sew?"

"Not a seam nor a stitch; I even insisted on it that the sewing machines should rest. I knew they would not sulk so badly in the fall. The strawberries you shall have as long as they last. The sugar and the cream we are sure of for the whole summer, if the cows do not die. And Mr. Pancoast tells me that there are seven of them."

And Rachel did a good deal as she was told. She helped Mrs. Vaughan to wash her nicest glass and porcelain in the morning—pet extravagancies, she said, which she would no more trust to a servant's care than she would trust the washing of a baby. Then it was, after a little, Rachel who rearranged the flowers. She made Tom bring her wild flowers, and that droll old Donald from the greenhouse gave her his orders, and suffered himself to be twisted round her finger. If Rachel fancied they would like to have her read aloud, she staid and read. But if the womankind dropped into letter-writing, she would be off alone in her canoe. She sunned herself in the sun, she aired herself in the shade, she thought a great deal, she read a little, she pretended to read more. She gained strength, and, without knowing it, gained spirit, and was much better prepared for the battle of life, wherever battle might be delivered, or whenever it might come.

Tom Poore said he had disinterred at the hotel a dried-up little Professor Radetsky, who was an accomplished pianist, and who had that curious Polish or Russian philanthropy, that he was never really happy unless when he saw young people dancing to the music of his own hands.

This was Tom's rather rosy account of the professor's predilections. The truth was that Tom had observed that, whenever the ladies danced at Lake Constance, some one was sacrificed at the piano for the others. At a suggestion from Tom to a business correspondent in Chicago the professor had been hunted up. It was true that he did not dislike an outing. It was also true that his delight was playing the piano. At Tom's invitation and expense, therefore, he was now spending the rest of the summer at Lake Constance. But Tom would have blown his brains out had he revealed this arrangement to any one, and this the professor, who, for that matter, was not in the least talkative, knew perfectly well.

One evening Mrs. Vaughan had asked everybody to ask everybody to come round to her house with a view to dancing. And among the children of light came the professor also. They were all resting after a dance, and the professor was playing some rather weird strain, perhaps of his own—perhaps a Hungarian gypsy dance.

"Yes," said Rachel, "there is no use in wishing, but I wish I could play one half as well as he does, and liked to teach other people only one quarter part as well as he says he does. I have been talking to him while I ate that sherbet. I declare I envy a man who is so well pleased with what he has to do."

"And what should you do if you had these gifts and graces?" asked Tom Poore, in reply.

"Oh, then my destiny would be clear. I should go to some new-fledged Chicago, some Tadmor in the wilderness, howling for a music teacher; I should hang up what you would call my shingle ; I should be the Professor Radetsky of that rising community.

"On Sundays I should play 'Hebron,' and 'Duke Street,' and 'Peterborough,' for the people to sing by, on the organ, and with terrible thunderings I should play the Hallelujah Chorus for a voluntary when Easter came round.

"Oh, yes, I should then have a vocation."

"You speak as if you had none now," said Tom Poore, afraid of his own courage, but also afraid to ask questions.

"Ah me! you are quite right. It is my avocation to be a fine lady at Mrs. Vaughan's. It is a very pleasant avocation to paddle my dear little birch. Nay, for an avocation, I was willing yesterday to stitch up that awful hole in the bark and to anoint it with wax and tar and to clap on a bit of bed-ticking. But no one will hire me to do that for eight hours a day, three hundred and twelve days in the year. There are not so many canoes in the Northwest as I could mend in that time. It is a good business, but, as I observe you men of affairs say, there is not enough to pay."

"And what is your vocation to be, failing a rival to poor Radetsky, and where is it to be exercised?"

"That depends," said the girl, trying to smile ; but Tom Poore saw, to his dismay, that he had annoyed her. And she, who did not mean to make a scene, was more annoyed that he knew she was annoyed ; so she rallied herself by an effort and went on quite equably :

"The truth is that in my heart of hearts I know I shall not teach anything else better than I shall teach music. I failed miserably in my Sunday-school teaching. It is in Sunday-school teaching, the most critical of all, that boys and girls are put in as apprentices."

"That is because it is so easy for some people to make other people good," said Tom Poore, recovering his usual courage.

"Yes or no, as it happens. I always begin with a large class, summoned by some skilful teacher who preceded me. The next week half have fled; the next week it storms furiously, and there are none; another week two come; and the last Sunday there is one little girl, who says meekly that she should like to sit with the others."

Tom so wished that he dared say that he should like to be the one left in her class, but he had not come quite to that point of audacity. There was, however, a moment's pause, and then he did say—that he might say something—

"After all, such things are generally determined for us. I am a manufacturer to-day instead of being a lieutenant in the navy, because my older brother's nose bled on his way to school."

"Perhaps they are directed for us," said Rachel. "But for women the tyranny is that we are all made teachers whether we teach well or ill. At bottom that is what all this howling about woman's rights comes to. We want more range of choice. But I am talking you out of all patience. Mr. Radetsky finished his sherbet long ago."

Why did not Tom Poore say to her then that there was one other choice open to her? Why did he not tell her to come and reign over him and his, as born and elected and sovereign queen? He asked himself that question many times that night as he walked home and after he was in bed, and answered it in many ways.

The real answer was that he was afraid. "Be bold, be bold, be not too bold," he said, as he wound his watch that night. If Rachel Finley had not favored this proposal and had told him not to follow this plan further, his vocation in Lake Constance would have been at an end. His chance might be better, he knew in his heart, if he waited longer than it was now.

For he saw the truth with a painful modesty for which few men or women gave Tom Poore credit. The truth was that while Rachel was pleasant and "nice," good-natured, nay agreeable, with him whenever and wherever he joined her, she was not in any way specially gracious to him. Not in the inclination of an eyelash! Not in the movement of her little finger! If they were all on the plank, ready to hand the ladies from the boat, she gave her hand just as readily to Crehore, or Bumstead, or Clarke, as she did to Poore himself. Not more readily, there was that comfort. But actually you might think all these bearded men were a string of school-girls, for all the distinction which this queen of women made among them.

"Right or not," said Tom Poore, as he tumbled into bed, not to sleep for hours, "what is done is done, and what is undone is not done." And the end of that sleeplessness was simply the determination again made, that he would stretch his arm far and wide to provide her with anything for which she expressed a wish; he would watch these last weeks of Lake Constance, and make them pass as brightly for her as might be; he would be the guardian genius, the slave of the lamp, who should care for her path and her rest. And perhaps she would find out that it was her vocation to trust herself to such a friend.

And this Tom Poore did. The *Rundschau*, and the *Cornhill*, and *L'Art* lay on Mrs. Vaughan's tables. Dr. Lapham's treatise on the buffalo mounds appeared from Milwaukee. Betham Kint, the queer outlaw, turned up every second day on the Vaughans' piazza, with fresh prairie flowers. The ladies all gathered to welcome him. But if Rachel Finley had not been there Betham would never have left his accustomed ways. The outside of Rachel's life was certainly well provided for by a friend who kept himself sometimes invisible.

CHAPTER XI.

PARTING.

> "Farewell again! and yet
> Must it indeed be so, and on this shore
> Shall you and I no more
> Together see the sun of summer set?"
>
> *Barry Cornwall.*

ALL the same, September would come. Betham Kint's flowers were more and more asterish and goldenroddy. The evenings were too cold for the boats, even under the bravest and most romantic admirals. What was more to the point, the grain of the country began to move. America began to give to half a waiting world its daily bread. And these princes from Milwaukee, from Toledo, and from Chicago, who, for all August, had been pretending they had nothing to do but to respond to the fooleries of wives and daughters, began to go about that great business of the feeding. It would be announced that Mr. Calrow had had a despatch from his head clerk: Mr. Armitage had taken the night express: Mr. Wells had sent a long message, but Mrs. Wells expected that they must all go to-morrow.

The end had come.

"It is very provoking, Miss Finley," said Tom Poore, "and I must seem to you very stupid. But Christern has mistaken my despatch, or else I made it too short. He has sent me Moritz's short stories, as I bade him, but he has sent them in the Hungarian original. Perhaps you read that also. But what I promised you was the German."

"Promised!" said Rachel, frightened. "You promised nothing. I thought you said you had them. Why, Mr. Poore, you know I should never have dreamed of your buying them."

It was true that Tom Poore had said he had them, if the English language was able to express that idea. But this was in Tom's general notion, that whatever was in New York was his, " to the extent of sixpence," as Mr. Carlyle well says. He would not have said that he owned Mrs. Stewart's palace or the Astor Library, but he was apt to think that what was for sale at retail, in Broadway or elsewhere in New York, was kept in the warehouses subject to his order. And so indeed it was.

Poor simple Rachel had her eyes a little opened by this incident of the Hungarian novels, and so she was rather on her guard when Mr. Poore went on to say:

"Of course, I can have them from Berlin in a few weeks. Tell me your address, and I will send them to you by post."

You are too fast, Mr. Thomas Poore. This young woman has seen quite too much at Kearsarge of the correspondence of girls with what is called, in the most vulgar of vulgar phrases, "gentlemen friends." She was not going to be betrayed into any such bother.

"If I knew my address, Mr. Poore, I could tell you. But I may be in Alaska, I may be in Cienfuegos, I may be in Boothia Felix. It is just as the one of these places or another needs a teacher with my exact accomplishments—a girl who can teach addition but not subtraction, is strong in multiplication but doubtful about the rule of three. There is room somewhere, if one only knew where."

And Mr. Poore saw that she did not mean to have him address any short notes to her, growing, by gradual evolution, into long letters.

The conversation would not lead up as he had meant it should. And once more his intrepidity gave way.

In truth, Rachel's name was in two "Teachers' Bureaus." These are places where on one side of the room are pigeon-holes full of letters from mothers who want governesses, and colleges which want professors, and school committees who want schoolmasters or schoolmistresses, while the other side of the room has a rack, quite as large, full of the letters of men and women who wish to be employed in such various services. These letters are accompanied by the "recommendations" of the applicants, and there is a photographic portrait of each applicant in the envelope with his recommendation. Ah me! if all the committees had seen Rachel's pretty photograph, she would have had no lack of applications.

At last the fatal Friday came on which the whole Vaughan party were to abandon the post as quietly as they might, and steal away to New Altoona. At this moment Rachel had in hand a promise from Miss Dudley that she might rely on the next assistant's vacancy at Kearsarge. She had also the refusal, for two days more, of the post of first assistant in the Seven Oaks Academy of Cuthbert County, Arkansas; and, lastly, if she wanted to take the district school in Hitchin, where she had submitted to Miss Hannah Valentine's loving sceptre, dear Mr. Tyndale held that open for her till the 15th of November.

But neither of these applications was to be accepted.

Quite to Rachel's surprise, on Thursday evening, Mr. Hutchinson, whose house was next to the Vaughans', asked her to come out on the piazza with him before he finished his farewell call.

"Miss Finley, my wife tells me that there is talk of your going to Arkansas to teach?"

"I was asking Mrs. Hutchinson about Arkansas. I am offered a place in a school there."

"Do you mind telling me what they will pay you?"

"Oh, not at all," said Rachel, though she was a little surprised; for Mr. Hutchinson seldom came from Chicago, and she supposed he hardly knew her by name in the crowd of young visitors at all the houses. "They offer for the first year three hundred dollars, with my board and washing." Then she added, with a laugh a little forced, "If the school fills up, I am to have more another year, if I stay."

"Miss Finley, I want an assistant book-keeper in our dressmaking department. You would be on duty from nine till four, and your lunch will be sent up from the kitchen. We should pay you eight hundred and thirty-two dollars a year, and you may take two outings, of a week each, when you wish. Miss Stoddard, the head book-keeper, is a fool, but she understands her business, and you need not quarrel with her unless you want to."

Mr. Hutchinson was taciturn when he spoke to ladies, and for him this was a very long address. Rachel was thrown off her guard. First of all, she said, "Some Frenchman says that if you are more than thirty yourself, it is quite convenient to have a fool for a chief."

Mr. Hutchinson smiled, well pleased. But Rachel went on: "You wholly mistake me. Your wife is so good a man of business that you think we all are like her. Now, in fact, I know nothing of book-keeping; I hardly know the difference between a cash book and a ledger."

"As to that," said Mr. Hutchinson, "Miss Stoddard knows too much. She is so scientific that she keeps me in hot water all the time. You can write a good letter, and you can divide two hundred and sixty-seven by eleven. That is all I want. I saw your letter to my wife yesterday about the book club.

"If you please, it is my business to judge of the qualifications of the people I employ. I have told you what the salary is, and what the outings are, and you have supposed you knew what the duties were. In this you were mistaken."

Rachel was snubbed, and knew she was, and said nothing.

"Let me tell you," said Mr. Hutchinson, girding himself up with an effort. "I want somebody in those rooms to keep the run of those girls. There are ninety-six of them to-day, there may be a hundred and twenty-five next week. There will be three hundred if Mr. Tileston say so; or if he say so they would come down to fifty. Now, I want somebody to see to them. Not to their sewing, that is Miss Fillebrown's lookout; not to their wages, that Miss Stoddard will see to, and, as I have said, will see to only too well.

"Miss Finley, if I should tell these girls that you were put there to protect them against Miss Stoddard, and against Miss Fillebrown, and against themselves, and against each other, you would not be able to touch one of them with a ten-foot pole. I mean they would be so shy of you. People never want to be helped officially by a person appointed to help them. But if you are there, rated as an 'assistant book-keeper,' these girls will bring you their grievances. If you are not a fool—and I think you are not—you will gain their confidence very fast, and I shall find that I am not killing one girl without meaning to, and also that I am not keeping another girl who is no good to me, or disgracing me.

"Miss Finley, my wife has done no end of good to these girls, who are not a bad set by nature ; but Mrs. Hutchinson cannot do everything."

Mr. Hutchinson was astonished at the length of his own harangue.

"Let me talk with Mrs. Hutchinson," said Rachel. "If she thinks I can do this thing, I will gladly try. I do not teach well, and I should be sorry to disappoint those Arkansas trustees by a failure."

So Rachel took Mrs. Hutchinson into the breakfast-room, and they had a long conference.

Things ended in her going to Chicago, where she was in fact rated as "assistant book-keeper." And the various bureaus of education will have, I suppose, her photograph to the latest day.

CHAPTER XII.

THOMAS'S CONCERT.

"The many rend the sky with loud applause ;
Love lost his crown, and Music lost the cause."
Dryden (revised).

HER life in Chicago was, of course, as different from life at Lake Constance as was life in the Gloucester fishing-smack from life at her Aunt Ann's. The first fortnight was clear sheer wretchedness. A new boarding-house, selected by Miss Stoddard to fit her own tastes—and those tastes were very unlike Rachel's — this was wretchedness double refined to a girl who had lived either at Kearsarge or at Aunt Lois's. The mere vulgarity and pretence of the place drove her wild. Her work in the half counting-room, half office, between a jealous chief who feared she was to be ousted, and a pack of a hundred girls, who did not know her or care for her, was anything but simple, or, indeed, intelligible.

"Do not come to me for orders," said Mr. Hutchinson more than once in substance. "I do not know myself how you are to do it. I only know that you are to be a friend to these girls and supply brains where they are needed. Find out your own way."

After one day of signal perplexity, in which she had wished herself in Arkansas fifty times, Rachel returned at night, tired to death, to the tawdry splendors of what was called her home, to meet at the door a grinning black girl, who said she had a card for her—" a gentleman had called, miss." In the two weeks of Rachel's stay here this was the first visit she had received from any person.

She took the card with some curiosity, therefore, to find it was Mr. Thomas Poore who had visited her.

He had written with his pencil that he would call again at seven.

And at seven Rachel had to receive him, in the back parlor. Seven other people were present in that room and four in the other. The conversation of all the eleven fell into silence, lest they should lose any word of what passed between the new boarder and the distinguished stranger.

Tom Poore was equal to the emergency, as to most emergencies. His conversation might have been printed in the Chicago *Times* of the next morning, and very probably was. It was on the most general themes—the health of Mr. and Mrs. Vaughan, the fortunes of young Walter Hutchinson, the probable bankruptcy of the hotel-keeper; and, at last, even the ranks of the listeners found the conversation unprofitable, and they began to retire one to his room and another to her newspaper. When the very last eavesdropper had thus departed, Tom Poore said quietly to Rachel:

"I ventured to call so early, on my way to my cousins', to ask if you would not join our party to Thomas's Concert. Mrs. Scroop is going and Mrs. Alderney. I have four tickets; will you not use one?"

"I had so wanted to go," said Rachel, "and I had no courage to go alone. Yes, I will go so gladly. You are very kind."

And she ran to make her preparations. Tom Poore

had a carriage at the door, and in triumph well concealed bore his prize away.

Nor had he invented Mrs. Scroop or Mrs. Alderney. These rather commonplace people appeared in the flesh— in a good deal of it, indeed. They showed no surprise that they were going to hear the music, nor gratification, nor regret. There were some who thought they slept during the performance. But who shall say? Their seats, as it happened, were one side of a passage-way, and Tom Poore had unbroken conversation with Miss Finley on the other.

Poor girl! she had not known how homesick she was. She had not really known how intolerable the boarding-house was, nor how maddening the desk and the work-room were. And here was music, and such music; and in the pauses, simple fresh memories of the lake, and the white lilies, and the canoe, and Cecilia, and summer days, and jolly evenings. It was a bit out of a lost heaven.

How soon—too soon—it was over!

But it was over. And the carriage was found again, and the cousins were lifted in, and their home was reached, and they were lifted out.

And Rachel was alone in the carriage with Tom Poore.

She knew Tom Poore liked her, but she did not dream of what was to come the very moment the door was closed and the order given for 939 Montana Street.

"Miss Finley, I may find no other place or time to speak to you. I have thought of you every hour since I saw you. So far as a poor blunderer like me can pray, I have prayed God to take care of you. You will not let me write to you, which is all right. And so I have come to Chicago, simply to say to you that man never loved woman as I love you, and to ask you to teach me how to make you happy. Oh, Miss Finley, if you knew how lonely and desolate this fortnight has been! And if you knew me, Miss Finley, you would know I never failed a friend."

Poor Rachel! Had not the fortnight been lonely and desolate to her?

Utterly lonely and hopelessly desolate!

But, even as he spoke, Rachel knew in her heart that in all that desolation, when she had wished she were at Hitchin, when she had wondered whether she ought not have gone to Arkansas, when she had gone over every minute of life at Kearsarge, she had not very often remembered that poor Tom Poore was in the world.

And now Tom Poore wanted to marry her.

"Oh, Mr. Poore, you must not say this. You do not know me. You do not know what a goose and fool I am."

"I know you are the first woman I ever saw who taught me what that word means. It is simply true that I have loved you as man never loved woman."

Rachel had often thought of marriage. She had never thought it foolish or unmaidenly to think of marriage. She had a hundred times found out that there were questions she could not answer, and duties she could not perform, and she had believed that a man, were he the right man, could and would help her through such perplexities. But all this did not help Tom Poore. Rachel summoned up all such memories, as the carriage rattled on, in two—three minutes, when neither of them spoke. And the memories did not help him.

"I see you are terribly in earnest, Mr. Poore. But it cannot be—it cannot be. Nor do I know why you thought it could be. I am so ashamed of myself if I have deceived you. But indeed, indeed, I am wholly surprised. Tell me you believe me."

And as she turned to look at him they passed a street lamp.

Her face was wet with tears.

"Forgive you!" he cried, "there is nothing to forgive. From the moment I first saw you as a little girl, to this moment, you have been a perfect woman. If you do not know that that is what you are, let me—let me have the poor privilege to tell you." And then after a pause, "Do not tell me that I may not write to you, now?"

"You may write to me, Mr. Poore—write if you please, but, indeed, indeed, it cannot be."

Tom Poore waited two days. Then he wrote from the Palmer House. It was a good letter, too. But Rachel simply answered:

Rachel Finley to Thomas Poore.

"Tileston & Hutchinson's,
Chicago, Oct. 1, 1884.

"Dear Mr. Poore: Think no more of it. It cannot be.

"Yours greatly obliged,
"Rachel Finley."

And with such spirit as she could Rachel went back to Miss Stoddard's jealousies and to the worries of the girls.

CHAPTER XIII.

THE ANCILLARY ESTABLISHMENT.

> "Busied at the loom, she wove
> An ample web immortal, such a work
> Transparent, graceful, and of bright design
> As hands of goddesses alone produce."
> *Odyssey (Cowper).*

It was in the next May that as Rachel Finley passed Mr. Tileston's door one morning, he called her in.

"Here is some handsome work, Miss Finley. These are *portières* for the club-house of the Knights of St. Melice. We have just received them from New York. The gentlemen are not quite ready for them, and have asked me to display them here."

Magnificent the *portières* were, and more than magnificent. Whoever had drawn these designs had been an American to the core. Clearly this was woman's designing too. The tall Indian corn which shot up from the ground on one, the play of the scarlet oak which waved down across the blue on the top of another, the cluster of cat-tails on a third, and the dragon-flies chasing each other on a fourth—all told of life in the open air. And the regulated freedom of the whole, the indifference to what may be called convent conventionalism, with the willingness to accept the restrictions of common-sense, were alike remarkable.

"Mr. Tileston, I have seen nothing which approached this. This is a new art."

"I knew you would say so," said he, well pleased. "The Knights gave me *carte blanche*, and I did not choose to disappoint them."

"Will you tell me what you paid for them?"

Mr. Tileston named the sum. It startled Rachel, even though she had set her own figures high.

At the end of fifteen minutes she sent this note to Mr. Hutchinson:

Rachel Finley to Ammi Hutchinson.

"Monday morning.

"DEAR SIR: Have you seen the beautiful *portières* which are in the show-room?

"I think the firm should know that we have in the building at this moment women who can do work quite as fine as this, and that the manufacture would not cost one third of the price you pay for them.

"Respectfully yours,

"RACHEL FINLEY."

"And who is to design your curtains, Miss Finley?" said Mr. Tileston good-naturedly.

"That is for you gentlemen to say. Ask Mrs. Langhurst to send you a design. Ask any of the artists. Or, if you will, try me."

"We will do all," said Mr. Hutchinson. And he did. But the truth was that the professional artists consulted did not take very kindly to decorative art. Rachel did. She had taken kindly to it since she lived with Aunt Ann, and had her first sight of things which have since been consigned to the chamber of horrors. There were a dozen magnificent houses in Chicago where cordial men and sympathetic women were glad to show her what had been done in other places. But Rachel had notions of her own. She did not want to repeat other people's experiments, nor did she.

As she had told Mr. Hutchinson, she had in the shop women who had been trained in every school of needle-work known. Convent training, Kensington training, Munich training, Antwerp training, Parisian training— Rachel had it all, or knew where to send for it within a radius of two hundred miles. And of experiment first and of success afterward, the result was, that in a little more than a year after Rachel accepted doubtfully the position of "assistant book-keeper," she was forewoman of an independent establishment, or one almost independent of the original Miss Stoddard room. Mr. Tileston, who loved his joke, called it an "ancillary" establishment. Rachel supervised. She designed. She ordered her satins and her silks. She found, to her surprise, that she was considered to have a good executive faculty. Her salary was doubled, and she was left quite free to work her will in what was justly called her own affair.

"Yes," she said to Miss Dudley, as she finished the letter from which most of these facts have been collated, "I am, on the whole, glad now that I did not wait and take my chance to come to you. But there have been times, oh how many, when I would have gladly scoured your knives and forks both for a whole term, if only I could have escaped from my daily conflict. Now I am queen, so far as my little kingdom goes."

And in her little kingdom she reigned and was happy. She made friends among the workwomen, into whose pretty work, naturally enough, the law of selection brought some accomplished and charming people. She made friends right and left in the open-hearted, hospitable, social circles of Chicago. The second winter was much more endurable than the first.

Orders for it flowed in freely from the luxurious palace homes which are scattered all through the great empire States of what was once the North-west.

As Rachel sat at her desk one morning opening these letters, she found, to her surprise, one marked "Personal," in a hand quite unknown to her.

John Wolff to Rachel Finley.

"Huddleston's Shaft, April 30, 1886.

"My dear Miss Finley : It is only to-day that, by a very happy accident, I have learned your address. I am able, therefore, to relieve the mortification which I have felt, when I supposed that you thought that I was neglecting my promise to you.

"For I have not chosen to believe, what is perhaps the more probable, that you have forgotten me and my promise."

So far Rachel read. And you and I, reader, who have the fortunate password by which we enter that office-door unheralded and unseen, can see by the flush on Rachel's face, very slight but very real, that she had not forgotten Mr. John Wolff, whatever might have happened to his promise.

The letter goes on :

"Do you remember how suddenly we parted on the top of Mount Kearsarge ? Alas ! I have long looked back on that thunder-cloud as something more terrible than we fancied it."

Did it kill Miss Fiske ? This question, which crosses the reader's mind as we exhume this letter, crossed Rachel's as she read :

"I went across to the seminary the very next afternoon, but I learned the sad news which had taken you to your old home. I was unable therefore to renew the conversation which Mr. Dunn broke off so suddenly when he called me to clean his kettle for him."

"How well he recollects details!" said Rachel to herself. But the poor child was equally conscious that she remembered them just as well.

"I took the liberty to visit you at Hitchin so soon as the term broke up at New Padua, but it was to learn that you had gone to Constance the day before. I addressed you at Constance, when I should have said 'Lake Constance.' My letter went to Boone County, Kentucky, remained there three months, and when I was in England was returned to me in New Padua, where it waited, I suppose, three months more.

"When I returned from England I went to Lake Constance to find a Persepolis of colonnaded hotels inhabited chiefly by bats and owls.

"To-day I have the good fortune to see your name in the Chicago *Times* as designing the curtains for Mrs. George Logan's house in Tecumseh. I write, in the certainty that there is but one Rachel Finley.

"For I ought to say to you, as soon as I can, that in England I had the pleasure of visiting Appleby, where I spent two days. I met many persons there who had the tenderest recollections of your father and mother, who were profoundly interested in the sad story of the Baikal, and who, indeed, made a friend of me because I shared those experiences with them. If you are Miss Finley of the Baikal, I shall have great pleasure in sending to you letters which I have lately received from Dr. Balfour and from Rev. Mr. Parry, who is still the vicar at St. Ann's.

"From Appleby I went across to Bishop Wearmouth, intending to call upon your Aunt Ann. I had obtained her address from Dr. Balfour. But in the very week of my arrival, as you probably know, she had sunk under an acute attack of pneumonia. I did not like to press a visit on Miss Sarah, your cousin, and left the day after the funeral.

"I took so much pleasure in my visit to Appleby, and have derived so much from the letters I have had since, that I am eager to thank you for an introduction which secured me a reception so kind of the best type of English hospitality.

"I was in England on mining business, in which by good luck I succeeded.

"The consequence is that I am established in my business as an attorney and 'general counsellor' here in a new mining town in the Rocky Mountains.

"Believe me, dear Miss Finley, your old friend,

"JOHN WOLFF."

To tell the absolute truth—and what else is the duty of this author?—the arrival of this letter was not an entire surprise to Rachel Finley; and, which is more, it gave her a great pleasure. If one may say so, she was annoyed that she was pleased. She had been annoyed for five years that she thought of John Wolff as much and as often as she did. But how was she to help herself? She could not think of her father and her mother without thought of the Baikal. She could not think of the Baikal without thinking of the way she left the Baikal. She could not think of that without thinking of Mr. Wolff. To have met him—to have seen him with the eye of the flesh on the top of the mountain, had given her great pleasure. Mingled with the pleasure was curiosity. Who was Miss Fiske, and what were her relations to Mr. Wolff? Rachel had asked herself these questions also, and had asked them more often than she liked—or rather these questions had asked themselves.

Dear Miss Dudley, dear Miss Haverstock, principal and associate principal at the seminary, I fear you disapprove the questions. I cannot help that. Truth is truth. I cannot tell a lie. The questions came, and had often come.

Rachel wrote John Wolff a letter. It was very short, but it was a very good letter. She did not write it for two days. Then she said, "I am a fool." And after she had written two orders for filoselle and one for gold thread, and I know not how many for chenille, she chose some nice paper, which had not the firm's heading, and wrote the letter.

Rachel Finley to John Wolff.

"11 Vinton Avenue, Chicago, May 7, 1886.

"Dear Mr. Wolff: I have your kind and interesting letter. I cannot thank you enough for your goodness in visiting Appleby, nor can I tell you how glad I am that you found the dear old place hospitable. I had not heard of Aunt Ann's death. They have ceased writing for some time, or have perhaps lost my changing address."

Before Rachel went on she waited half an hour. She had an interview with Mrs. Mattoon, as it happened, about some very elegant hangings for the Sorosis of Hotwater. In the intervals of Mrs. Mattoon's meditations Rachel meditated not on corn-color and saffron, but on the second half of her letter to John Wolff. When Mrs. Mattoon had elected one corn-color and one saffron, as foolish people will, so as to be wholly sure that they are wrong, Rachel applied herself to write the other half. She was conscious that she wrote under difficulty.

"I do not know how to thank you for your kindness in visiting Appleby and Bishop Wearmouth. Your letter brings back what begins sometimes to seem like a dream. I am glad to know that there is somebody in the world who believes such places exist. More than once I have asked the gentlemen here to lend me the *Times*, in the hope that I might find the dear old names; but I never find them, even in the Corn Market.

"And I am so glad that you saw Mr. Parry and dear Dr. Balfour. I knew they would not forget me.

"If you can spare their letters for a few days, I will keep them carefully and return them at once. I think you have given me courage to write to Dr. Balfour.

"Believe me, dear Mr. Wolff, gratefully yours,

"RACHEL FINLEY."

She did not write this second part without remembering that when Tom Poore, good fellow though he were, had offered her a novel by Maurice Jokai she would not let him send it to her.

It is true that a Hungarian novel is not a letter from Appleby.

How if John Wolff had offered to send a Hungarian novel?

This question crossed Rachel's mind.

But she did not answer it.

In five days after Rachel had sent this letter she received a large "registered" letter, the second which she remembered to have received in her life. This did not contain a certificate of stock. It contained several photographs of public buildings in Appleby, a portrait of the well-remembered face of Mr. Parry, the clergyman, and several notes and letters from him and Dr. Balfour to John Wolff, which showed quite distinctly how that gentleman had advanced from the relations of a stranger interested in the local antiquities to a near acquaintance amounting almost to intimacy.

If John Wolff thought that he should give Rachel exquisite pleasure in sending this parcel, he was quite right. Pleasure mixed with pain. Yes. That is the way with pleasure. But the parcel gave to Rachel a very happy evening.

Two days after, late in the forenoon, she was on her knees in the designing-room, just drawing in upon a magnificent fold of crimson satin the leading lines which were to guide one of her most skilful needlewomen, who was to fix the exquisite forms of a handful of water-lilies upon the curtain. The door behind Rachel was thrown open, and the Swedish girl who ran her errands and attended her bell said, in her outlandish dialect:

"A gentleman wishes to see you, Miss Finley."

"All right," said the unconscious Rachel, supposing he was where he should have been—in the office. "Bid him take a chair, Thekla."

The stupid Thekla withdrew, and John Wolff stood silent behind the unconscious artist.

He did not care to interrupt her. She poised herself on her left hand, which was gloved. She worked with charming freedom and promptness with her right, varying her chalks from moment to moment, which lay in a saucer on one side. One and another lily started from the rich groundwork. Once and again she looked up at a great basin full of the pretty creatures which stood on a chair at her left. But she had clearly a very distinct notion of what she was about, and what she meant to do.

When she had thrown half a dozen of these graceful forms upon the satin she struck a hand-bell which was on the floor, rose to her feet lightly, and stepped back to see the effect.

"I beg your pardon," said John Wolff. "I believe the girl should not have brought me here. I did not mean to interrupt you."

If he had dropped from heaven Rachel would not have been more amazed. It would be fair, indeed, to say that she would not have been so much amused.

She recovered herself in a minute, blushing very prettily all the same.

"Have you been here ever since Thekla spoke to me? I thought a Mr. Sullivan had come ten minutes too early for his appointment, and that he was waiting in the office. I did not mind making him wait, for indeed I am very punctual. But you have been standing all this time? Pray, come in."

And to make up for her neglect, if neglect it were, Rachel was perhaps more gracious, certainly was less reserved, than she might have been to her unexpected visitor.

His visit was but a broken one, of course. Mr. Sullivan came, and Mr. Wolff had a chance to see how Miss Finley dealt with a man of business.

Madame Leger came, who was to embroider the water-lilies, and Rachel bade him come to advise with them about one or two doubtful points.

Then they would begin on Bishop Wearmouth, and some eager girl would come running in to stigmatize the twist of some silk or to consult on the foil to a color.

John Wolff had tried his bold experiment, and he had to satisfy himself that it had not wholly failed.

"When may I see you when I do not interrupt you?" he said. "Are you at liberty this evening?"

Rachel was at liberty, and fixed the hour when he might call.

Oddly enough, when he called, he asked her if she would like to go to Thomas's concert. For Thomas and his belongings were in Chicago again. Rachel assented, and they went. There was no carriage, and no talk of a carriage. And though the distance was full two miles, Mr. Wolff's only allusion to it was to ask Rachel if she preferred to walk. She said she did, and they walked. Oddly enough, I said, but the real oddity was that when they came to the hall, where Rachel had not been since she came with Mr. Poore, their tickets happened to be to the identical seats, or so she thought, which she occupied with him on that evening when she was so happy. Did she make all this up as she went along, as Miss Dudley had taught her Bishop Berkeley supposed?

And they walked home. What did they talk of? I know, but I will not tell. They talked of everything, from the heavens above to the earth beneath, and to the waters under the earth. They did not think they knew everything. They knew that they did not. But they felt of every conceivable subject, in that happy range of opening confidences when neither of two people is afraid of the other, when each is willing to confess ignorance, and when both are willing to wonder, to ask questions, and both hope to know more. That Rachel had come by intuition to some of his most cherished convictions of life and duty was to John Wolff an exquisite pleasure. That this man, thirty years old, who had seen life on the frontier, while he talked of Mr. Gilder's poems and of Aurora Leigh, should own himself still a learner in so many things, was to Rachel a surprise. To talk, squarely and fairly to talk, of two hours and more on things of the Idea ; to live with another sympathetic friend, as eager as she for the larger life, not simply while she read some magazine, or heard Mr. Batchelor preach, or sat before her evening fire with Mrs. Browning—this was a new luxury to the director of the embroidery of Hutchinson & Tileston. And Rachel was distinctly conscious of regret when the long walk was over and they were at home.

"You would have preferred to take the car?" said poor John Wolff guiltily. "I was very careless."

"Indeed no, Mr. Wolff. You forget I am a country girl. I owe you a very pleasant evening."

"I wish you would give me one to-morrow. At what time may my cousin call on you?"

And his cousin called—a frightened, dowdy, silent mother of a family from the Blue Grass region of Kentucky. "Fetich," Mrs. Winchell would have said, and "Fetich" it was. But that call was supposed to give John Wolff some additional privileges in the way of escorting Miss Finley to one public place or another, and, indeed, in calling upon her in her pretty parlor in Vinton Avenue.

"Why Vinton Avenue?" he said to her one day.

"I asked the same question when I came here, and was told that my question showed the ingratitude of republics. It seems Mr. Vinton was a great statesman, and he was born in sight of Kearsarge Seminary."

CHAPTER XIV.

HUDDLESTON'S.

" Oh for a lodge in some vast wilderness,
Some boundless contiguity of shade."
Cowper.

AND after three or four days of life gilded thus by sunset glow and evening starlight, John Wolff returned to his new Potosi in the Rocky Mountains. He returned to ask himself whether by any miracle this lovely woman, who had found her own foothold in the world, would abandon it to share his foothold with him. He did not live in a log-cabin. Oh, no! The house he lived in was builded of sawed lumber. An ell behind was the original log-cabin of the first hero, Huddleston, who in prospecting had struck his foot, one happy day, on that fated stone which had rolled down from the cliff which had yielded the ore which the shaft had sent to the smelting mill at Yorkville, and which Yorkville distributed to the world.

Streets had extemporized themselves on the line of the trail by which the lonely Hod Huddleston brought his morning pailful of water in those days of prospecting, and by which he went down to the creek or up to the "clearing." A church had built itself where he tethered his two burros, when he became rich enough to have them, and a school-house stood at the corner where he had first blazed a tree-trunk when he trod this wilderness as its discoverer.

Such was the novelty of the place where John Wolff was the leading magistrate and attorney. He held in his hands, when the court came in, more "briefs," if anybody had called them so, than any three of his friends at the bar.

It was to this wilderness that, when he went to Chicago, he had audaciously hoped he might induce Rachel Finley to remove—to bring her dear, sweet self and to be the glory and treasure of his life.

And he had found Rachel Finley herself, in her way, a leader, a power in the world in which she lived. He had almost forgotten the wilderness as he had sat in her pretty parlor, as he had breathed in the fragrance of her fresh roses, as he had read to her Tennyson's poem from the last Continental magazine, as they had talked of Ruskin's notions of clouds, and of Mr. Tyrwhitt's drawing clubs. He had been bold enough, before he went, to think of dragging this charming woman to share with him this shanty in which he lived.

He was not so hopeful now.

But John Wolff knew, from the hair of his head to the sole of his foot—he knew that he loved this woman with a love that quickened every pulse of his life. When it began he could not tell. He certainly was not conscious of such a mastery over every hour of his life, when he lifted a wet, laughing girl out of the Atlantic, or when he spread for her his ulster in the stern sheets of the Baikal's cutter. Had he been, three years after, when he and she met, day by day, on the piazza at Greeley's at Waterville, that day when he piloted the party up Osceola—did he know then that she was to have this empire over his life? John Wolff looked back over it all and wondered, and could not tell himself. Certainly he had thought of her ten times as often as he thought of any other woman in the years between. Certainly, that day when they were talking on Mount Kearsarge, he would have rather cut off his hand than go and help Dunn with his old kettle. When did this mastery of a man by a woman begin?

And what was it? Certainly not that she was the most beautiful girl he ever looked upon. John Wolff said to himself that he had seen many other beautiful women, though, of course, there was no one quite like her. Her smile? or her way of talking? or was it that she was so frank and threw you off your guard?

John Wolff turned it over and over as he rode day and night and day and night from Chicago to Huddleston's Shaft, and John Wolff could not tell.

John Wolff turned it over as he sat in his better room in the shanty which had been built in front of Hod Huddleton's cabin, and again he could not tell.

Nor can this author tell. Only this: that it was quite certain that Rachel Finley was the queen of John Wolff's life.

And where was the queen to reign if he should bring her here? Alas! there and then it was that John Wolff saw and felt the deficiencies of his surroundings.

For a thousand dollars Merriman the carpenter would put him up a better house than this. But hardly on a spot so accessible.

And she, living in luxury there in Vinton Avenue, in such quarters as Merriman the carpenter never dreamed of!

Poor John Wolff! Could he have the face to ask his queen to reign in such a palace?

A knock at the door.

"Be you the Squire?"

"Yes, I am; come in; there's a post and chain round the corner. Fasten your horse. Will not the lady come in?"

"That's jest it," said the man, relieved because the young Squire's foresight saved him from the necessities of further explanation.

"Yer see, she had to walk up from the depot, and I met her at the Crossings with the burros 'n the little cayoose—that's Nahum's. Nahum lent her to me; he throwed her, 'n got off to the creek, 'n I had ter go after him 'n catch him, 'n ride the blasted critter myself, 'n that's wy we're here so late, 'n we must be ter hum 'fore sundown. Nahum's my pard."

As he gave this somewhat unnecessary explanation, the lady herself entered. Her aspect and that of her dress confirmed his account of the difficulties of her journey.

John Wolff suggested vainly that they had better go to the Elder's, a quarter of a mile farther on. He was obliged to say that he knew the Elder was absent at the moment at a miner's funeral, but Mrs. Primrose would tell them when her husband would be home.

"No more waitin' for me, Squire. I have been waitin' long enough already, haven't I, Lucindy?"

And a ready smile from Lucindy confirmed the statement.

John was fain to make them stand up on one side of the office, and with as much solemnity as was possible, in a form well-nigh as brief as the English language would permit, he made them one and gave them his blessing. Brief though the ceremony was, before it was over there were several admiring witnesses who entered the office after it began.

They gave little time for congratulation, nor indeed did the parties most concerned seem to care for this. The new-comers thronged around John Wolff to explain to him that the one-eyed Welshman had hit Yankee Pete over the head with a shovel and had fled ; that Pete was bleeding profusely and was supposed to be dying in his brother's cabin, and that John's services and especially his seal were necessary for the rapid completion of a will which Pete desired to make before he died. Almost superstitious reverence was attached in this community to a few printer's types encircled with a bit of bent brass rule, and all mounted in a grotesque handle of laurel-wood which was in John's possession, transmitted from his predecessor. "Et's the old seal of Arapaho County, 'n 'as been for years, sens the fust pilgrim come up from St. Louis. Et was good then from the British line down to New Mexico, and et's good in the same country now."

Before John had finished with the will he thought he might be needed to hold an inquest. But, on the arrival of his professional brother on his way back from Mulligan's, where three men had been crushed by a landslide, it was made clear that Pete's injuries were not fatal. Messengers were despatched with instructions to those who were pursuing the Welshman that if they were not particular his life might be spared ; and John, after executing Pete's will and hiding it in a certain tobacco-box indicated by Pete's brother, returned to the meditations which had been somewhat suddenly interrupted. Again he looked sadly around the inner office. As he rode from Chicago, it had been easy to imagine that with a little care it would be made to equal the pretty sitting-room and kitchen of the Elder's wife. That would not be like Rachel's parlor. But nothing could be like

Rachel's parlor. It would be neat and decent, and he should not be ashamed to bring her into it. Some improvements he could make, and would. First of all, the four prints which were the decorations of the wall should not be tacked to it with carpet-tacks when the queen came in. They should be framed, and framed by his own hand.

So he went back into the shed which served as a workshop, lighted a tallow dip, and stuck it carefully upon a sconce on the wall, and selecting a bit of yellow pine went happily to work on something which should remind him every minute of the woman whom he loved.

Happily he had worked for more than an hour, though the time seemed shorter, when he was called into the office by loud cries and sturdy knockings; and, appearing with his candle, was greeted vociferously by a dozen friends. They were clothed all in leather, and wet from top to toe, and muddy as they were wet; but every man was loud and glad with cheerful congratulations, which John did not understand for many minutes. Whenever any person who had any sense attempted to explain, a new crowd of eager visitors broke in at the door, and with their hand-shakings and vociferations silenced the well-meant beginning.

But at last a lamp got itself lighted, the greater part of the company found seats on the benches which were used for witnesses in occasional trials, the rest disposed themselves on the tables, and George Fletcher, who was recognized as captain of the crew, was permitted to tell their story.

Fletcher had been away for four days as the delegate at a State convention. The Territorial Government was to give way at last, and this convention was to name the officers to be voted for in the new administration. It had been pretty well understood who all the important candidates would be, and Wolff took no interest in the return of Fletcher—who was professionally sometimes his antagonist, sometimes his associate, and always his friend—but in the certainty that he would bring in a little new-made gossip from the capital. But Fletcher had indeed news to announce. For just as the convention was finishing its labors it was announced that Judge Sargent, who from the beginning had been a favorite in the Territory—had indeed once held, as his own, the famous grand seal of the unbounded county of Arapaho —had been thrown from his horse in fording a river and had been drowned. The convention had, of course, named him as the candidate for chief justice. But so soon as the news of his death came, it had been necessary to slide up on the ticket the names of the other judges and to place upon it one new name.

"And George, he nominated John Wolff! Three cheers for George Fletcher! Three cheers for John Wolff!" Six cheers were given lustily. By this time all the population of the Shaft were in or around the office, and it was clear enough that, whenever the election came, no man would be permitted to vote for any one but John Wolff in that precinct.

"George; he hit bed-rock that time! Three cheers for George!"

"Sheer madness," said Wolff, when they gave him time to speak. "I wonder they heard you through."

"They did hear me," said Fletcher proudly, and well pleased with his maiden success, as well he might be.

"I think you know me. I said enough, and I said no more. I bet on the best horse, and the best horse won."

"Three cheers for the two-year-old!" This was the

cry of one of John's enthusiastic constituents. By some accident it was quoted afterward, and for twenty years he was affectionately known as the two-year-old in all that county.

John would not treat, excepting to tobacco. Every man of them knew that when he came, but none the less did a crowd, constantly renewed, of loyal adherents throng the office till long after midnight. It was in the densest smoke, after two o'clock in the morning, that John found his way to the bed on which full fifty of his supporters had sat in turn, in the last six hours, to reflect as he might, and to thank God as he could, for the unexpected.

When he waked that morning he could offer to the woman whom he worshipped, to the queen of his life, no better home than such a barrack as this he lived in, and such a future as depended on the duties which that afternoon he had been rendering to Law and Order.

To-night, as he went to bed, he was certain that he could offer her a home in the town which was to be the capital of a growing State, and for seven years at least an income which, if not large, was certain, and which would be quite sufficient for all his modest wants, and, as he dared hope, for hers. Such a woman as Rachel might not care, but John Wolff cared that the social position which he asked her to share with him would be second to that of no person whom she would meet or see.

Oh, if he could think that she thought of him once while he thought a thousand times of her!

What would she say when he wrote to her, as he should do as soon as the sun rose, to say that his future was assured; that all he was, and all that he had was hers, and that the happiness or the misery of his life was in her hands?

CHAPTER XV.

CHICAGO REVISITED.

"Love whispers in my ear his trembling strain,
Which I with trembling lip repeat to him again."
Petrarch.

As the rosy light of morning made even the rough hillside above the Shaft beautiful, John Wolff sat at his desk and began his letter. He did not owe Rachel a letter. Not he. He had used up all his rights the hour after he returned from Chicago, under the pretence of sending her a scrap which he had cut out from an English newspaper, and had before forgotten. But at this time he had that supreme right which every man has, at least once in his life, in his dealing with woman. Rachel might be surprised, when she received a second letter from the Shaft so soon after the first. John could not help that. Surprised or not, she would not put his letter into the fire.

John Wolff to Rachel Finley.

"HUDDLESTON'S SHAFT.

"MY DEAR MISS FINLEY: I hope that my letter will not surprise you. I hope you have some idea of the feeling which I have long had for you, but which I have had no right to express till to-day. Yesterday morning I could not have written what I write now.

"If you have seen that I hold you in the highest

esteem, you have seen only what you have seen in a thousand other men. If you have guessed that I love you with all my heart, there has been at least some introduction made for this letter. But I have done my best not to offer any addresses which I had no right to offer. Until yesterday I had no home to offer to any woman. One of the queer chances of frontier life now offers me honorable work to do, and a position more than decent, such as I have a right to ask you to share. No place in this State can be made into such a pretty paradise as you have made around yourself, and I feel painfully enough how mad I am to ask you to share with me the roughness of our life. But if you ever need a strong arm and a true heart, here they are. And if, as the books say, love can make any home happy, yours shall be the happiest in the world.

"Whatever your answer to a letter so bold,
"I am always yours,
"John Wolff."

No, in the bottom of her heart Rachel was not surprised when this letter came.

But, in truth, she was troubled when it came. This good fellow did not know her, and she knew that he did not know her.

Heavens and earth, what was it all! They had not really talked with each other twenty times in their lives. Those woodland excursions at Waterville, that half-hour on the hemlock boughs at Kearsarge, the evening at Thomas's concert, the day in Mr. Tileston's yacht on the lake, the morning when they went to Mr. Batchelor's church, the little party she made in her own rooms for his cousins—these and the other incidents of his stay in Chicago had given him no knowledge of her. "How can the man take the risk of marrying a woman he never saw?"

Yet Rachel knew very well, from the first moment, that she was not going to write to John Wolff any such letter as she wrote to Thomas Poore. What she should write she did not know. That question she carried in her heart all the morning. In all the discussions with Miss Stoddard as to that knotty question about the advance of wages to the Klepstein girl, in all those serious instructions from Mr. Tileston about the Lyons invoices, the letter to John Wolff was in the forefront of her brain. At lunch, when all the heads of rooms were together, and when there was some special interest about the flowers they were to send to Mrs. Bartlett, Rachel's thoughts were far away in the Rocky Mountains. And when she went home, and Clare brought in her solitary dinner-tea, Rachel asked herself how such a meal would be served at Greeley, at Prescott, or at Jamestown. "This will do, Clare. You need not stay. I'll wash the things myself."

There is no excuse for a moment's more delay, Rachel. Here is paper on the Davenport, here is pen, and here is ink. The man is in misery, and you must write now.

Rachel Finley to John Wolff.

"VINTON AVENUE, CHICAGO.

" MY DEAR MR. WOLFF: Your letter has indeed surprised me, as you knew it would. Indeed, you do not know what you are doing. Your cousin thought I was joking when I said I was a fool and a goose. But I had said it a hundred times before, and it was never more true than it is now.

" Do not think me hard in saying so, but indeed, Mr.

Wolff, I do not know you, and how is it possible that you should know me?

"Indeed, you should know more of your wife, Mr. Wolff, than that she swims well enough to come out of the water when she has been fool enough to tumble in.

"You spoke as if some business might call you to Chicago again. If that happens, will you come and see me? I feel sure that I can then explain to you that you are quite mistaken in thinking of me as you do.

"In reading my letter, I see I have not said that I am honored; indeed, I am flattered by such confidence and regard. Pray believe that I am,

"Very truly,
"RACHEL FINLEY."

Thus did Rachel Finley evade John Wolff's letter.

Rachel, the woman who deliberates is lost. John Wolff received the letter at half-past eleven in the forenoon. At twelve he was on his horse. At five o'clock he was in the express train on the Union Pacific Railroad. Two days after, at seven in the evening, he rang the bell at Vinton Avenue, and absolutely to Rachel's surprise, Clare, who liked John Wolff, showed him in, unannounced, to her mistress's parlor.

"You sent for me, Miss Finley, and I have come."

"Mr. Wolff, I am so glad to see you." What was there in her eyes? John Wolff took not one hand, but both, and pressed his lips to hers.

"I should like to know this," said Rachel to John Wolff one evening, as they walked together under the moonlight in Lincoln Park. "Can any one tell me when and how all this began? I do not suppose that every man who fishes a little girl out of the sea falls so immediately in love with her."

"That depends," said John Wolff. "Anadyomene, the old people called her—one who rises from the sea."

"They never called anybody so who had on a water-proof and a storm hat and india-rubber boots. Even your audacity will not pretend that it began then."

No: John's audacity did not pretend that it began then. But John did now carry the beginning far back in that blessed visit of a fortnight in dear Waterville. And it proved, as they came to talk it over, that Rachel had a very accurate memory of parties to the Elephant, and the visit to Swazey's pasture, and the first lessons in trout-fishing. It was agreed that, while foreordained in heaven, "it" must have begun at Waterville. And to dear Waterville they agreed they would make a pilgrimage, when first they could take a journey eastward.

"And I declare I have wholly forgotten one thing," cried Rachel. "I meant, I should have asked it first of all. Whatever became of Miss Fiske?"

"Miss Fiske? Who is Miss Fiske?"

"That is just what I ask you."

"Miss Fiske? There is old Ann Fiske, who fries the pork and washes the clothes for the boys at Gresham's Gulch. You don't mean her. She must be Mrs. Fiske, I think. I always supposed she was very much married."

"What nonsense!" cried Rachel, who was, however, laughing till she cried. "I believe you are keeping something back from me. I mean the pretty Miss Fiske who blushed so sweetly when we surprised you at her feet on the side of Mount Kearsarge."

"Whose feet?"

"Miss Fiske's feet. You do not forget your idols so

completely, do you? When you take young ladies up mountains, and sit at their feet, and whisper soft nothing in their ears, you do not forget their names, do you?"

"Do you mean—you do mean—Tom Dunn's half-sister, the man with the kettle?"

"I do not know whose sister she is. I know she seemed to be under your care."

"Under my care? That girl under my care? Tom Dunn had two sisters there, I believe—one was named Dunn, and the other one—do you say her name was Fiske? I should have thought it was a longer name. Is it not Waters? I never saw her before, and I never saw her again. I have not thought of her from that hour to this."

Poor Rachel believed him, and only did him justice in believing him. But she was conscious that she had thought of this mysterious Miss Fiske a hundred times.

And John could not stay, even in that kingdom of heaven. Just then and there for these two the other name of the kingdom of heaven was Chicago. But there was much writing back and forth. The postmaster at the Shaft came to expect one of Rachel's pretty letters every day. And it was settled that, as soon as the election was well over, the new judge should come to Chicago and Mr. Batchelor should make them one. John had found a better house in the mushroom town which had been made the seat of government than he had dared to hope. As to furnishing it, Rachel would not let him give a thought or say a word. That, she said, was the business of the lady and the lady's friends.

"Have I not fitted out half the grand brides in Chicago?" she wrote to him. "Whether our hangings in the kitchen shall be mauve or crimson I have not yet determined. But I have determined that you shall not select them nor pay for them. You write like a madman. You seem to forget that, besides the accumulation of my honesty industry, I am a stockholder in the great New England Stocking-Loom Company. I have only to sell out, at the present favorable rates, and not a house in your baby capital shall be so well furnished as ours. You may bring your own benches and stools. Pray bring the pretty picture-frames. They shall hang in our best parlor—that is, in the only one. For the rest I shall provide."

And provide she did, and that very prettily. Her business tact came into play, and the arts of Chicago were well illustrated in this pretty home in the new metropolis.

John's election was triumphant. Indeed, the whole ticket had been well framed, and there was no organized opposition. It is not in the first days of a new State that party feeling shows its worst.

And the week before Christmas Mr. Batchelor married them. There was a quiet little party in the Unity Church, and then Rachel bade good-by to her kind Chicago friends. After two days' travel she appeared as Mrs. Judge Wolff in the new capital. She could not but remember, as she rode from the station to her new home, that other drive, not so very long ago, when every tree was a curiosity and every corner of a road a novelty, as she rode from the station in Hitchin to Aunt Lois Winchell's.

And so began seven years of life which Rachel always looked back on afterward, not as the happiest, perhaps, but as in a certain way the most notable of her varied fortunes. "I was such a fool, you know," she would say. "Yet people were so good to me, and certainly there is a Providence which takes care of fools." This merit is there in these new places, that everybody alike is inexperienced. There is no fashion. Every woman is a law unto herself. "My dear," said Mrs. Justice Trustum to Rachel when she made her first visit, after she had expressed her frank admiration, so that Rachel blushed, "My dear, you are the etiquette. Have it just as you choose yourself, and there is no one of us privileged to say you are wrong." Best of all, Rachel's children came to her: that wise girl, who was to be one day her mother's dearest companion, and who, when she was three months old, would look out from her great eyes as if she saw all the mysteries in earth and in heaven. Then, not far apart from each other, followed two hardy and uncontrollable boys, who in after days would worship this sister with a fond idolatry, but who in these infant days of the new State occupied themselves chiefly in clamoring for food and devouring it.

Here was where Rachel's heart was; here was where nine tenths of her life was spent. Looking back on these years afterward, here were the eternal hours which stood out in memory, so that no passage of time changed them. But the people of the town knew her rather because she loyally did her part of the work which comes on the leaders of such a place. The congregation outgrew the church. The men were willing to have another built, but what with smelting and prospecting and digging, what with building roads and bridges, what with flumes and reservoirs and other works of irrigation, there seemed very little chance that the men would stop to build the church. The organizing and raising subscriptions and writing to architects seemed to fall very much upon the women. And loyally the women did their share, Rachel among the rest. Then the graces of life were to be kept up in all this rush and whirl. The book-club was to be organized, the Society of the Red Cross was to be ready. When an avalanche swept all the houses on one side the stream at Holliday's down into the lake, when there were forty-three children who rushed home from the school to find that they had no mothers and no homes, then the Red Cross was ready to reply to the telegraph which announced the calamity. Morning brought its people to the spot, perhaps hundreds of miles, with the clothing for these children, with oversight for the orphans, with food, nay, with homes for all. Such was the work of the Red Cross, and of the Red Cross, almost of course, Rachel was treasurer.

They had, before two years were over, a very pretty opera-house, built by one of those mysterious agencies which provide opera-houses for all the world more promptly than any Extension Society provides churches. Occasionally a travelling troupe hired it for "an entertainment." But the best entertainments were those provided by home talent, and the best people in the town knew that in proportion as home talent maintained them, they would be kept out of the hands of irresponsible directors. So Rachel, and the Judge too, for that matter, lent a hand in the Shakespeare Club, and in the Dramatic Union as well. Whatever would make these people look aloft was good for these people. And John Wolff and Rachel did their fair share in seeing that the town should grow in the right way, and, while it was growing so, should not drift in the wrong.

CHAPTER XVI.

THE CRY IS STILL THEY COME.

"More guests arrived!"
—"Then show them into the banqueting-hall."
Hunchback.

THE Red Cross Society had met for an unusual meeting. The regular meetings were held once a month. But news had come by telegraph this morning that the whole village of Meldon had been burned the night before, and this night was the second day of December. Three thousand people were homeless, or nearly so, where yesterday was a pretty, thriving town. Meldon was thirty miles from the rail. Whatever was taken to the place must be taken on the backs of mules and horses after it left the train. On this news the Red Cross had been summoned and had met in full force. The meeting was called in the parlors of the Methodist Church, but so soon as it proved that they were overfull, the Presbyterian ladies had gone across to their church and had started their fires, so that a meeting of equal size was in full blast there. Rachel and Mrs. Taggart, Mrs. Trevino, and Mrs. Trustum were of course at the fore.

Rachel was giving her orders.

"In the storehouse under Flint's we have six barrels of hard-tack, that pork which came back from Hatchett's, and one cask and two cases of boys' clothing.

"Mary, make a memorandum and give to Mr. Willis.

"You will find the key, Mr. Willis, at Flint's, and I think the railroad people will take them on the evening train if you say it is Red Cross work. Have you force enough to handle them, Mr. Willis?"

"Certainly, Miss Wolff; there is not a young man in town but will lend a hand."

"Very good; then send me four young men who have heads on their shoulders, can read and write, and will not talk more than half the time to my young ladies here. I will not bother you any more, Mr. Willis. Good-by, and thank you ever so much.

"Laura."

"Yes; here I am!"

"Put on your hood and boots. Mary, write this despatch for me for the telegraph:

"'Station-master at Eglinton. Forward by night express to Hatchett's all the stores you have belonging to Red Cross which can possibly be of service at Meldon.

"'RED CROSS.'

"Laura, if a woman takes this there will be no charge. If they make any, pay."

And Laura went. And so on. And so on. The bended bow had gone out at nine in the morning. All day the energetic chiefs and their loyal retinues had been at work to meet the sudden demand. The Military Academy had sent down canned meats, the warehouses of the Bellerophon were thrown open to the Red Cross order, etc., etc., etc. The whole city knew that three thousand people were to be fed, perhaps transported to a new home. The city had not to organize any staff for such a purpose. The Red Cross was always ready.

The express passed at quarter to six. Fifteen minutes before, Mrs. Trustum in the Presbyterian Church, and

Rachel in the Methodist, dismissed with thanks their hearty coadjutors, and with the promise that the bells should ring in the morning if the Red Cross needed them again.

Then Rachel took home with her Mrs. Schumann, a little German lady who had come over from Auburn to join in the work, and Mrs. Le Sage, who had come up from the mills in the same way, and whom Rachel had persuaded to spend the night with her. To complete the tea-party she asked Grace Harding and Jane Seaver. "Alexander and Charles, when you have locked up, come round and join us at tea. Mrs. Trustum has promised to bring in her young ladies in the evening."

With these hospitable words Rachel locked the door of the church, mounted to the front seat of her sleigh, and took the reins. The snow was falling faster and faster. It had been falling steadily since noon. She drove down the avenue to find at her own door the public conveyance from the railroad—a vehicle half coach, half sleigh, close covered—from which her husband's head and in a moment his full form appeared.

"What good luck brings you home, my dear John?" cried the astonished wife, well pleased.

It proved that a bridge on the branch line to Ashland had given way, and that, rather than wait in the train perhaps twenty-four hours for its repair, the whole bench had come up, together with the travelling lawyers, who had joined the circuit. Of these Judge Wolff had brought with him two friends, who were to stay at his house, and whom Rachel welcomed cordially.

She hurried her own party into the house, welcomed the well-known friends of whom the Judge had spoken, and then discovered, for the first time, that in his party was also a French gentleman, a savant who had brought letters from New Padua to her husband, and whom he had met on the train. Rachel's cordiality was inexhaustible, but she was a little frightened when she found that he did not speak twenty words of English, did not understand ten, and that she must bring her modest French out from its retirement.

With her husband's aid she lighted the parlor; she whispered to Grace and Jane, who knew her house as well as she did herself, as to which room they must take the gentlemen. She sent hot water after them, and summoned her two friends, Mrs. Le Sage and Mrs. Schumann, into her own bedroom.

"I cannot give you as grand quarters as I meant," she said, "but you will not mind."

Nor did they mind, but with all the sweet good breeding of the best Western hospitality gave themselves up to the business not merely of welcoming these strangers, but of making everything pass simply and easily. When the French savant wrote home he gave to his wife the impression which he had himself received, that the house was twice as large as it was, and had a staff of invisible servants.

As soon as Rachel's young friends, Charles and Alexander, came in, she bade one of them telephone to the Military Academy and ask Professor Hackett, the teacher of natural history, to come down and to bring George Barber with him, and anybody else who could talk French, or anybody who cared for botany.

When Dr. Decandolle appeared after his ablutions and the other requisitions of his toilet, Rachel gave him over, in her own best French, to Mrs. Le Sage, who was only too happy to be his guide, philosopher, and friend. Mrs. Le Sage and her husband were both from the coast on the river above New Orleans, and she spoke with that pure French of the best Creole families which is always a delight to exiled Parisians, travel-worn and long-suffering.

Rachel gave some general directions in her kitchen, and left them to work themselves out by their own evolution.

As a matter of course Jane and Grace, who had come in only as guests, took the part of assistant hostesses as soon as they found that this flood of unexpected visitors had poured in. Rachel, indeed, never thought of asking them to take this post, nor did they think it necessary in form to offer. They loved her and she loved them—that was enough. They saw that their services were needed, and those services they gave. No etiquette compelled, but on the other hand no etiquette hindered. And, exactly as in the morning they had gone to the relief of the people who had been burned out at Meldon, so they now came to Rachel's relief when her hospitality was so severely tested.

In an incredibly short space of time the table in the dining-room was stretched to its full length and prettily arranged. The best china had been designated by the Indian girl in the kitchen, and had been nicely set in such a way as pleased Grace's eye; and Jane had sent one of the boys, as she called them, across to her father to cut such straggling flowers as he could find in her little conservatory, lest the Frenchman should feel solitary for lack of something that was alive. Biscuits and "tea-cakes," in forms not to be described by this modest pen, piled the board with lavish luxury, while cold meats and hot oysters, two thousand miles from their cool birth-places in the Chesapeake, provided substantial refreshment for those who had travelled two or three hundred miles since morning, as some of the guests had done.

Just as they sat down, Professor Hackett and two or three of his pupils appeared, one of whom was the George Barber whom Rachel had asked for. Before they came into the parlor a good deal of clatter and laughter could be heard in the hall, and this was explained when they came in. The snow was gathering so fast that they had doubted about their return. They had all come down therefore on snow-shoes—not necessary, perhaps, but convenient. It was the fun with which they explained this, and the noise made by stacking them under the porch, which had made all this row on their entry.

All this was unfolded in detail by Mrs. Le Sage to the wondering Dr. Decandolle, who was at that moment turning over a portfolio of French etchings, which, as he told her, he had never seen in Paris. "Ah, my friend," he said in reply in his own language, "I shall never understand your country. At one moment and the same I am in Paris with my friends, Jacquemart and Flameng, and you talk to me of shoes for snow in words which belong to the—what shall I say?—the shores of the wilderness. I am like a voyager in the icebergs, who lands to study a crevasse, and he finds the flames of the tropics."

At which moment the Professor was happily deposited at the table at Rachel's left, and, as he found his place, lo! two or three branches of blazing Euphorbia, which Alexander Mitchell, with a hand rather too free, had cut from a fine shrub he had found in Jane's little conservatory.

"It is impossible," said the man of science. "It is all a dream. You do not tell me that the Poinsettia is to be found among your evergreens at this season! I came to study cactuses, and I find pines. I study pines, and you show me—"

But at that moment the Ute girl from the kitchen, who was attending that end of the table, and had just given the unconscious botanist his coffee, came round into his full view. She was the first full-blooded Indian he had seen. High cheek-bones, raven hair prettily dressed with a bit of scarlet ribbon, a head curiously set on the shoulders, a curious heaviness, not uninteresting, in the movement of eyelid and eye—all characterized a race with which the man of science was not in the least familiar. Nor was the position the less queer because the girl was offering a pretty cup and saucer of French china to Mrs. Schumann. The Professor's speech broke down, as he would have stopped talking had a butterfly wholly new crossed his path in the woods, or had he come across an orchid in the Bois du Boulogne. He looked at the other end of the table to see if there were any more specimens, possibly interested in hearing the conversation of the race. And there was pretty Jane Seaver standing behind young Mitchell with a silver salver, offering him some muffins and joking with him as she did so. And the Professor subsided for an instant, and was hardly understood when he said to Mr. Le Sage:

"I am reminded every moment of a geological paper of my friend Agassiz on 'the impossibility of reconciling the American stratifications.'"

"Stay with us long enough, Professor, and we will teach you the law."

And now Mrs. Le Sage found why George Barber had been sent for. George Barber not only spoke French eas̄ly, but had made a study of the local flora of the region for a hundred miles round. He was in correspondence with the Smithsonian, and, through them, with half the rest of the world. So in two minutes he was answering the Professor's questions, solving his doubts, and was in a fair way to provide him with five years' good occupation in the mountains and cañons. Alexander Mitchell had given the academy party a hint of the company they were to meet, and Professor Hackett and George had brought down with them two or three portfolios of dried plants, with which, as the evening went on, they were able to illustrate their scientific conversation.

The Professor, who knew that his arrival was not expected, was as much amazed by this rencontre as he was by the blaze of the Euphorbia. He had not become habituated to the telephone, and seeing that these gentlemen joined the party about the time he did, he imagined that they also were accidental guests. Unconsciously, therefore, he credited the average citizen of the State with the range of scientific information, not to say with the ease in the French language, which these two gentlemen showed. Nor, if it had been explained to him for a week, would he ever have understood that if he had not come they would not have come, but that they had been selected by his hostess as the best she could find for him.

They lingered, as well they might do, after their day's experiences, over the tempting table. When at last they had regained the parlor, just as there was talk of some music, more guests appeared, and proved to be Mrs. Trustum "with her young ladies." They were a group of pretty girls from Milwaukee who were visiting at her house, and they also had been lending a hand in the labors of the day.

"But, Rachel, I do not think you know what a storm it is. The girls put on their boots, but there was not one of us who could wade to the gate, and if we had come to it we could not have opened it. I made John Gyer harness his horses, and we have all ridden. That will go into history. 'The celebrated snow-storm in which Mrs. Trustum was obliged to drive across the avenue.'"

And the girls looked very pretty and rosy after their exposure to mountain weather.

But where was Judge Trustum? He had not been on the circuit with the other lawyers.

The Judge had gone to the hotel to call on some English gentlemen who had come in from the West and brought him letters. "I told him if the gentlemen were young and nice, to bring them here. But I told him if they wanted to talk about wills and reversions and chancery and pokery, he might stay at the hotel. But, whether any of them come here, whether they do not spend the rest of their lives at the Meriwether House, I am doubtful. In that case we will spend ours here."

Nor did this seem such an unhappy outlook when one saw the delighted Professor lecturing about ferns to delighted hearers, Mr. Wendell and Mr. Fay well pleased to talk with Mrs.' Schumann and our pretty Grace Harding, the Academy lads sorted out with the Milwaukee girls, and the other members of the company disposed to their minds. But it was not long before new trampling in the porch and hall showed that other guests were working in through the snow. Judge Trustum had found the new arrivals pleasant, and the arrangements at the Meriwether dull. He had sent his own carriage away. But in the covered sleigh which plied in all directions from the Meriwether, he had brought in Lord Widdington, a young English nobleman, who was making the tour of the world with his tutor and physician, Dr. Winkworth. To them the Judge had added, lest his party should seem incomplete, the celebrated Dr. Hammerstein, a German geologist, whom the host at the Meriwether had introduced to him. For this he apologized to Rachel :

"It seemed a little hard to leave him all alone, when we were all talking together there. And I knew you would excuse me. I telephoned to Lang, and told him if he looked in he would find the man here, so you will not have to entertain him."

Rachel assured the Judge that there was no need of apology, and in point of fact, Lang, who was the State geologist, came in in a few minutes. It proved at once, of course, that he and Hammerstein had studied together at Freiburg, and there was thus a meeting of old friends.

The young Englishman proved jolly and companionable. Dr. Winkworth was in his element, both with geologists and botanists. Mrs. Schnmann played when they wanted music, and when they did not she did not. Before long some of the young people asked leave to retire and prepare an impromptu charade, which Lord Widdington had seen done at Honolulu, but which they thought could be improved upon. So they were turned loose into the entry, and used the wraps of the guests for the wardrobe of their extempore theatre. With great success they performed, first Haec-Thor and afterward Bed-Lamb. Indeed, things went on so pleasantly at this improvised party that when the hall clock struck for midnight every one was surprised.

"Where in the world is John Gyer?" cried Mrs. Trustum. "Cyrus, do look out and see if John Gyer is freezing in the storm. I told him to be here at half-past eleven. Indeed, Dr. Winkworth, I have, as you see, to supply all the decorum and dignity for this company, in both the houses. These young people were dancing the German till two this morning, and to-night

I was to have tucked them all up in their beds before midnight.

"Where in the world is John Gyer?"

At which very moment a peal at the door-bell announced John Gyer. In an effort to work through the driveway from his own stables his horses had been stalled in the snow before he was well in the street. In their struggles to free themselves "the thills was smashed," as John put it, while the horses were still in the drift. John had done such work as he could to relieve them, and had finally with difficulty, which the snow on his person revealed, struggled across for help to John Wolff's house, where, as he knew, he could summon a force of men.

On the instant the most competent arrayed themselves for the duty. These were, naturally, the Academy boys, with their fortunate provision of snow-shoes. With these they would readily run across the five hundred yards—here six feet deep with light snow, there wholly bare—which separated the houses of the two judges.

The English gentlemen and the French and German naturalists, ready, like gentlemen, to be of service, stood, naturally enough, a little doubtful what service they were to render.

But John Wolff did his best to put them at ease.

"You must not think of your quarters at the Meriwether. Their man cannot come here, nor can you go there. You will not understand till morning how four quiet hours of snowfall can change the condition of affairs. Mrs. Wolff will shake down something for you to sleep upon, and will make you—well, as comfortable as if you were sitting bolt upright as third-class passengers when the train is not on time."

George Barber returned in twenty minutes. The horses were unhurt, so far as wounds went, and were back in the stable, where John Gyer was rubbing them dry. The sleigh was a wreck, and clearly it was hopeless to try the same experiment with another. Judge Trustum, therefore, had sent back Professor Hackett's snow-shoes, and had instructed George to suggest to Mrs. Trustum that she and the Milwaukee ladies had better spend the night with Mrs. Wolff.

"I do not see that Mrs. Wolff can help herself," cried Mrs. Trustum gayly.

Lord Widdington asked if they might not have one more charade, and, in fact, they had two. Then the party for the Academy made a start, in face of John Wolff's protest. In fifteen minutes they returned foiled. Mr. Hackett would not risk it, he said.

Two more charades; the clock struck two, and then Rachel sent them all to bed.

Who slept on the floor of the office, who slept on lounges in the parlors, who slept on buffalo-robes in the attic, it is no part of this tale to tell.

But never met a jollier party than the company at breakfast, when a sky of the deepest blue overarched a world buried in snow; and in various languages, and with a thousand jokes, Rachel's unexpected guests assured her that they never slept better in their lives.

As the last of the gentlemen among her guests bade her good-by, when the road-breakers had rendered any motion possible, Rachel turned to Mrs. Schumann and Mrs. Le Sage and said:

"So much for one day. Now we will see what another may bring forth. Susie, dear, bring your sampler, and Mrs. Schumann will show you how to make that W we bothered over."

CHAPTER XVII.

CLOUD AND STORM.

"After this, she thought she saw two very ill-favored ones standing by her and saying, 'What shall we do with this woman?'"—
J. Bunyan.

SUCH was one of Rachel's days. And of hundreds of days, each wholly unlike this, the history might be told.

John, of course, was away on circuit nearly three months out of four. In his absence Rachel acquired something of that poise and self-dependence which they say those charming daughters of Nantucket gained when their husbands, sons, and brothers were away on cruises three years long. To repeat the proverb which has been cited before, she could "paddle her own canoe." And when her oldest boy was five years old, he had persuaded himself that in his father's absence he was a material help in the fortunes of the family. As he filled his little cart with chips for the kitchen stove, Ephraim Tait, who was splitting the logs for it, addressed the boy to give him counsel in this matter:

"Doctor, wat ye're doin' 's in the right line. Wen you's five you's to hev a hatchet yourself. I told ye mother so, 'n she agreed. They's no use in ye goin' to school, doctor. I told ye mother so, 'n she agreed. Wen they's as many books 's they be in the office, it'll kinder soak in. I's often seen that. Books is nothin' to knowin' how to work young. I shall take keer of that, doctor. I told ye mother so, 'n she agreed. Pack the chips into the kitchen, doctor."

Little Bill, who had accepted since he was two days old the title of "doctor," conferred by Ephraim's University, gladly acceded to any theory of education which kept him from the kindergarten, to which Tom Trustum had to proceed daily. To tell the truth, Ephraim Tait had most of the qualifications needed for a skilful "kindergartner," had the experts in that affair had the wit to discover his qualifications. Rachel had.

But this little book is not written to tell the fortunes of a rising metropolis or of Rachel's children, but only the turning incidents in her fortunes. It was in the summer of the seventh year of their stay here that on the sky of their life, clear enough till now, there gathered a cloud, as big as a man's hand, which soon took larger proportions.

Rachel did not see the cloud from any window. Nor did she learn of the cloud first from the oracles of the *Daily Irrepressible* or the *Frontier Blackguard*, though before the cloud broke she watched for those signs of the times with feverish curiosity. Ephraim Tait first made her aware that any cloud was rising.

"I see Jem Stiles wen I was waitin' at the depot, 'n he sez, sez he, that old Trustum 'n the Jedge hed better hurry up thet decision, or they'd be kingdom come round the Court House. I told him to shet up; 'n sez I, ef you don't hold your jaw ye'll git chosen Jedge yourself, 'n then, sez I, wen you 'n Bollers go on circuit, sez I, they'll be two burros on one bench, sez I. 'N 'e shet up mighty quick, I tell ye."

Just what "kingdom come round the Court House" meant Rachel did not know, and she was quite too proud to ask Ephraim. A telegram had told her that her husband, whom she expected, would not leave Ashland for three or four days more.

So in her evening's letter she asked what "kingdom come" would be.

In John Wolff's note of reply were these words:

"It is pathetic enough, that you, of all the world, should not know of the creak and strain about 'Waddles *et al.* Trustees, in appeal *vs.* Cook and Hunter.' It is the great railroad case—of which you do know—and a crew of people have persuaded themselves that the world will come to an end if we do not decide the wrong way. It is really this decision which keeps us here, but it will not be read till I come home."

Such warning had Rachel, and only such warning, for a state visit which she received at eight in the evening the day before her husband was expected.

She had just heard the children say their prayers, and had run down-stairs to write a letter to Cecilia. Rather to her surprise one of the "hacks" from the Metropolitan Hotel drove up, and two stately gentlemen, not quite in the costume of the frontier, came to the door and rang.

Rachel answered the bell herself, as was the not infrequent custom in this capital.

A short, nervous, quick-speaking man, dressed with the utmost precision and bearing a gold-headed cane, offered her two cards.

"Ask Mrs. Wolff, if she will see Mr. Hudson and Mr. Tremlett."

Rachel recognized instantly the names of two of the great railway kings of that day—if indeed one do not say Moguls. She named herself, and showed them into her pretty parlor.

Mr. Hudson was quite too nervous for study of the scene. Mr. Tremlett looked round with interest on the prints on the walls, on the music on the open piano, with a little of the air with which Lieutenant Greely might throw a glance around the interior of the snow-hut of a hospitable Eskimo.

"We have come from New York," said Mr. Hudson, nervously, "on this business. And now I learn your husband is away."

"My husband is away, but I expect him to-morrow. Can you leave no message? What is the business?"

Message! business! Did this little woman really suppose that the critical twist in this Waddles and Cook matter was to be explained in ten words which might have been spoken on a doorstep? Certainly women are fools! Such, in substance, was the internal reflection of Mr. Hudson, and his first impression was that this particular woman must be suppressed, or, as he would have said, "sate upon."

"No, madam, I can leave no message. I have travelled two thousand miles because what I have to say is not of a character to be written down."

Rachel saw that he was enraged. But she did not know why. She did not very much care, unless she had made a blunder.

"I have a telegram from Ashland," she said. "The judges all leave to-morrow morning, and will be here to-morrow night."

Mr. Hudson smiled grimly. "Of those facts I was aware. My people in Ashland know that I have arrived. It will be necessary, as you will understand, I suppose, that I shall see your husband on his arrival."

"I know he will be very glad to see you," said Rachel, her thought taking instantly the hospitable turn. "Perhaps you will take tea with him—and your friend?—a little late I suppose the train will be. The Grand Sierra, you know, is too grand to be punctual." Then, with a wish to conciliate or relieve this anxious face, the unconscious woman added, "Are you quite comfortable at the Metropolitan? I should be so glad if you would send your trunks here."

"There are several of us, Mrs. Wolff, and we cannot well separate. Mr. Talfourd is with us, and Mr. James—perhaps you have heard those names—the most distinguished counsel in New York. We have thought that even the legal lights of the Rocky Mountains might not dislike to confer with these gentlemen."

What in the world was the matter? Rachel did not understand these oracles, only she did suppose that the arrival of Messrs. Talfourd and James meant "kingdom come at the Court House." Still intent on her hospitality, she said, "Pray, bring any of your friends with you. Judge Wolff will be very glad to see you all."

Actually this woman thought that the appeal of the trustees and the essential decision in chancery, on which turned the rights of thousands upon thousands of bondholders and stockholders, was a matter to be talked over between tea and coffee, as a question side by side with "Will you have plum or quince?" Mr. Hudson was wellnigh beside himself with this absurd Oread simplicity.

"I think that Judge Wolff will perhaps do us the favor to call upon us when he knows that we are here." This he said with all the dignity of millions.

"I will tell him that you are here," said Rachel, with some dignity on her part. She would have liked to say that in the mountains it was not the custom for the court to call upon counsel, however distinguished, but she bit her lip and said nothing.

Mr. Tremlett, who had been silent till now, was enough of a mind reader to interpret her thought. He had been annoyed from the beginning by the nervousness and consequent presumption of his companion. He tried to mend matters by saying, " Of course we do not expect any further legal discussion. All that Mr. Hudson means is a friendly call on our large party."

But poor Mr. Hudson, a grandee at home, and very much used to having people "stand round," as the vernacular puts it, was quite worn out by three nights of sleep upon the rail, even in his own private palace, and he took offence even at the words of his chief of staff.

"Friendly? Yes, I hope it will be friendly. I do not think that even* chief-justices would care to make war against the Grand Sierra and the Inter-Oceanic together. If they do mean war, it shall be war to the knife."

War to the knife! Was this man crazy? Rachel looked instinctively at Mr. Tremlett, and from his almost entreating eye received the instant signal which meant " Do not care in the least for what he says. You and I are allies, and we must both humor him." So Rachel answered good-naturedly, " Oh, you must not think of knives, Mr. Hudson, because you have come into the mountains. Indeed, I never saw a grizzly in my life. That skin your feet are on seems savage to you, but it is a present an old trapper made to my husband. It was really very funny, Mr. Tremlett. My husband married him seven years ago, and he paid no fee, and only last month he brought this skin to show his gratitude. But indeed, Mr. Hudson, there are very few grizzlies now."

So chattering, Rachel did her best, by as many separate points as she could, to draw the pent-up lightning from the cloud. Nor did she wholly fail. Mr. Tremlett caught at the cue, and almost to Mr. Hudson's surprise they were in another minute all talking about the benefits which the Grand Sierra had brought to the State. They were discussing Mr. Whitwell and Mr. Parker, the fine young engineers who were running the branch line to New Potosi.

"You must not send us many of such nice young men, Mr. Hudson"—this was Rachel's conciliatory speech. "All our girls are crazy to go on excursions to see the works, and the whole social life of the city is demoralized." As if the great Mr. Hudson had even heard the names of Mr. Whitwell or Mr. Parker!

It was not Mr. Tremlett's first experience in managing a crazy lion, and as for our dear Rachel, I believe she could have walked, like Una, among twenty of them, and that she would not have been afraid of them. She rang the bell, and the well-trained Ute girl, whom Rachel had picked up at one of the agencies, came in with a cup of tea and some hot muffins. The gentlemen did not know they were hungry, perhaps were not; but even to careless men there is a certain sacramental power in the breaking of bread and the passing the cup, and before the hour was over the great railway king was happier and more genial than he had been, since that horrid moment when a long despatch from his counsel had called him from his luxurious palace on the Fifth Avenue to a pretentious third-class hotel in a valley of the Rocky Mountains. Meanwhile, to his own amazement, "the driver" of the "Metropolitan hack" was pacing up and down the plank walk, wondering what these blamed tenderfeet from Chicago had to say to Miss Wolff to keep them so long.

To the driver Chicago was the farthest East.

Rachel's little French clock struck ten almost spitefully, just in the pause after a bright story by Mr. Tremlett of his experiences in Siberia. "How late it is!"

said Mr. Hudson, starting with real surprise. "Tremlett, we are keeping that carriage waiting. Will you see where the man has gone? I want to say a word to Mrs. Wolff." Mr. Tremlett left the room looking troubled, and as he closed the door gave Rachel that eager look of entreaty again.

To her inexpressible amazement, the great man took her hand and said, "I am afraid I was uncivil when I came in. I did not sleep well on the Plains. I am so glad to count you among our friends. Our correspondents spoke as if you were all our enemies."

"Enemies!" said the unconscious Rachel; "why, Mr. Hudson, you have not an enemy in the State. We all know what we owe to the Grand Sierra, and the very children named their sleds Inter-Ocean."

"I wish I thought so," said Mr. Hudson, flashing up again. "We must hope that that time will come. Meanwhile, as it has not come, and the lamb cannot lie down on the lion, I am glad you are on our side." Rachel stared, but said nothing.

"I was very angry," he continued; "perhaps I showed some signs of it. After my long journey, to find that your excellent husband was away. Indeed, we needed to consult him. Our advice here is not of the best. If it had been, things would not be where they are. But now, dear Mrs. Wolff, that we are such good friends, I shall go away sure that we have one advocate here. I hope we may have more. I can talk to you better than I can talk to any one." And he paused for a moment, and Rachel wondered whether he were stark mad. He did not seem to find it so very easy to talk to her. But in a moment he rallied.

"Some things are said better than written, perhaps. And then I am glad to know how engaging and successful an advocate we have with this stern judge, who has our destinies in his hands. I am quite sure he can refuse you nothing. Dear Mrs. Wolff, if it should happen next Thursday that he is not well enough to go into court, and if he decline to give an opinion at this term of court, while his nerves are unsettled, there will be fifty thousand dollars at your account in the Bank of the Metropolis in New York. And, if you can persuade him not to offer himself as candidate at this election, but to accept a retainer from us as our counsel here, he may be sure of that position."

He had to hurry these last words; and well he might, for Rachel had started to her feet and was even protecting herself by her chair, as if a wild beast were indeed before her.

"Do you insult me in my own house? Am I mad, or are you? Because money can buy iron and mountains, do you think it can buy men and women? You shall not speak another word to me," and she put her hand upon the handle of the door that she might take refuge in her kitchen and leave him alone. But the railway king detained her. "You do not see," he said, "you do not understand. You are in our power; both of you are in our power. All of you are in our power. You said we made this State. We did make it, madam, and we will take care to rule what we made. I tell you, madam, what your husband will tell you, too, that if he speak twenty words in Thursday's decision in such fashion as shall injure the Grand Sierra, the people of this State will send him tramping where he came from. Why, the people of this town will tear down this house about your heads if I raise my hand." Rachel was storming with rage. Her anger gave her that sublime power that she could pretend to be calm. "You bribe me in one minute, you threaten me in the next ; in both you insult me. Go out of this house. I shall not feel safe till I hear that door close behind you."

And the poor creature, though he were raging too, did as he was bidden.

CHAPTER XVIII.

CRISIS.

" The hapless husband and his bride shall stray
By night unsheltered, and forlorn by day."
Camoens.

JOHN WOLFF came the next night, as had been expected.

The train was late, as Rachel had said.

The crowd of loafers at the depot was twenty times greater than usual. Ephraim Tait had John Wolff's carryall waiting, and the Judge gave the Chief Justice a seat. It was clear to any eye that people, as it were, rolled back from them both, as if no one wanted to seem particularly intimate, though every man in the crowd would have shaken hands with either of them, or might have called either by some nickname had they been in favor, or had he " an axe to grind."

Cotterell, on the other hand, the third judge, was welcomed by a sort of ovation. Everybody wanted to shake hands with him. One man took his carpet-bag, and another his umbrella. He was almost carried to the Metropolitan coach, and so many admirers pressed into it with him that coachmen and porters had to remonstrate. The " gentlemanly keeper of the hotel" was at hand and addressed the concourse. " All come up to the house, gentlemen. Supper is waiting for the Jedge; but perhaps when he is rested he will make us a speech. We shall all be glad to hear him. But don't crowd the kerridge now—you can drive on, Hosee."

The Chief Justice and John Wolff, driven by Ephraim, retired silently from this scene of triumph.

"It is perhaps your first experience of unpopularity," said the older man. "I have tried it before now."

"But I fancy," said John Wolff, sternly, "that you never tried it when your enemy was organized and had twenty or thirty millions with which to create public opinion."

"Not quite," said Judge Trustum, "but in the old Arkansas days the whole planter power was a corporation without knowing it. Men hung together by the law of the instrument, if they owned slaves. They couldn't help it. It was as drops of quicksilver run together. Yes, the pressure then was quite as hard as it is now," he said, cheerfully.

"Let us hope that some day these people's children, if not they, may have more grit, so as not to be led by their noses by every fool, though he have a gold divining rod. But here we are. I suppose you will not come in. Take the Judge home, Ephraim," and Rachel stood at the open door to welcome him.

No word had she by which to worry him. The supper was all ready. The flowers were on the table, and little Susie had been kept up out of bed to see her father. Then they went all three up together to see the little boys asleep. Susie was put to bed, and they said their prayers with her. Then the two came down together, and each dreaded the five minutes that were before them.

So it was a fair relief to Wolff to find he had nothing to tell his wife, or that she had, in substance, the same thing to tell him which he had to tell her. The reader will have understood that the two great railway interests of that part of the world had come into collision. On this particular hearing in equity, which for years was to be familiarly spoken of as "Waddles and Cook" or "Cook and Waddles," depended the question whether the Interminable Company might or might not make a certain connection through a certain cañon. The Grand Sierra people had persuaded themselves that if this connection were made they would be ruined, and, by a thousand agencies well known to them and theirs, they had persuaded the press of the State, and naturally the people, that it would ruin the State. It had even proved possible to bring such influences to bear upon Cotterell, one of the five judges of the Supreme Court, that he had granted an injunction, ordering the Interminable Road to cease its work in this "Wild Cherry Cañon" just at the most favorable season of the year. The Interminable people had two or three thousand men there, and disobeyed. The sheriff had not failed to stand by the judge, the militia were ordered to the place, and had gladly rallied, and some bloodshed had already taken place. On an unimportant side issue, the case of Cook and Waddles had been brought into equity to be heard before the full court, but it was understood that all the rights and wrongs of the Grand Sierra on the one side and of the Interminable on the other were to be decided and stated. Indeed, this union of all the cases had been brought about by Wolff, who had sense enough to know that only shysters and speculators were trying to postpone a decision, and that the country needed peace, and for peace prompt declaration of the Law.

The great hearing had taken place at Ashland, because the full court was there. It was known, of course, that Cotterell would stand by his own injunction, having been, indeed, in the pay of the Grand Sierra when he made it. For this, neither John Wolff nor Judge Trustum, the Chief Justice, cared, except that the credit of their bench was injured by it. The full bench was five, and a unanimous decision by four judges would have just as much weight in the State where they were all known as if this poor creature had joined in it.

But to their horror and indignation, when the Court came in for the final arguments, Cottyngham and Bruce, the two other judges, said that they had private interests depending on the decision, and must not sit! The decision was thus left by these weak-backed brethren to the Chief Justice and Wolff alone. Both Cottyngham and Bruce had been "approached" in the vacation, and had been persuaded each to buy a share of the original stock of the Grand Sierra, at four dollars and twenty-five cents. What inducements they had for this investment, in itself unprofitable, no man knew, or told if he did know.

When Judge Bruce made this announcement of private interest, and gathered up his papers with some swell and fuss to withdraw, even the packed court-room at Ashland hissed him. The old Chief Justice, who had looked into the bores of rebel rifles without flinching, looked over his spectacles at him calmly, and then turned to John Wolff, who was left alone on his right:

"Brother Wolff, be good enough not to blow out your brains till we have finished this inquiry."

So the three remaining judges, Trustum, Wolff, and Cotterell, had gone through the long arguments. They had taken time to draw up the opinion, and this was the opinion for which Mr. Hudson, Mr. Tremlett, Mr. Talfourd, and Mr. James, with every living man, woman, and child in the town, were now waiting with such eager anxiety.

When the court met the building was crowded, and around it thousands upon thousands of miners, railroad workmen, and other people from twenty miles around filled up streets and squares.

After a tedious string of routine, which was hurried by as well as in decency it could be, the Cook and Waddles business came on, and the Chief Justice said that the decision of the court would be given on all matters together. He regretted that the court lost the counsel of two of its members; this the old man said with sublime scorn. He regretted also that the opinion of those members of the court who were able to sit was not unanimous. But it was the decision, and in an interlocutory way, as if to the general audience, the old man added that he supposed he need not say it was final. The opinion had been prepared, he said, by his associate, Mr. Justice Wolff, who would read it. "But," said the old man with energy, "every word in it has the absolute approval of the majority of the court."

So John Wolff read this critical opinion. Talfourd and James, the lights of the New York bar, listened intently, and with a secret delight which they were both too well trained to display, to its simple and direct statement of principle, of constitutional right, and of State law. Step by step it passed along, through the difficult mountains and the provoking molehills of the controversy. And at the close, with a lucid statement which left the Grand Sierra without one inch of ground, Wolff read the decree. In "Cook and Waddles" the attorney for the Grand Sierra were allowed a certain bill of costs, about which they were anxious, and for which they had contended. In that critical matter of the permanency of the injunction which restrained work in the Cherry Cañon, for which permanency the Grand Sierra had been contending, the court dissolved that injunction. "If the trustees so wish, that work may go on to-morrow or to-day."

Mr. Talfourd and Mr. James, the magnificent New York lawyers who were retained as additional counsel for the Grand Sierra, looked at each other, and each made a little inclination of the head, but they did not even smile. The old Chief Justice, with a certain irregularity which the crowd in the court-room justified, said to the people rather than to the bar, "In view of the popular interest in this case, I think it well to say that the people of that neighborhood should understand that this decree is final, and that, as before now, the whole strength of the State must be devoted to maintain law and order."

Judge Cotterell in the briefest form expressed his dissent, and then the court adjourned. It would have been hard indeed to do anything else. For, from the moment John Wolff sat down, a storm of hissing and hooting had made all that was said in order inaudible.

And thus was the spark put to the waiting magazine. The sheriff, who was a hardy old soldier and cared for hisses as little as he cared for grasshoppers, meant to keep order in his court. Before they knew it two of the men known as ringleaders in these clamors found handcuffs on their hands, and were marched into the cells down-stairs. In general the people in the room did not find this out till the sheriff had succeeded. But in this little triumph he had sent his four best men out of the way for a moment, and the howling and yelling were now fairly irrepressible. The judges retired, however, unmolested. It is but fair to say that nobody thought of delaying them. Cotterell went out with none of the ovation of the night before. People had forgotten him in that eager rage which asked what should be done next. And to various liquor saloons and other points of popular discussion they retired to consider this question.

Unfortunately the *Frontier Blackguard* was an evening journal. The temptation to sell a large edition to the people who had come into town was irresistible. The special grievance which the *Blackguard* harped upon, was the indignity offered to THE PEOPLE by the arrest of those two distinguished fellow-citizens, Dennis Malgruddy, Esq., and Hod Fitts, Esq., who by the minions of authority had been fettered and thrown into a dungeon for the mere crime of expressing the unbought sentiments of American citizens. The editor defied the Minions of authority to fetter him. He would be found in his office. But he ventured to inform the Minions that a six-shooter lay on the table beside him.

Now people really cared very little about the utterances of the *Blackguard*, and cared nothing for its editor. But, by misfortune, some one not quite drunk read this aloud that evening to a hundred men who were quite drunk in Gus. Mitchell's "Free and Easy." A proposal was made at once that the company should march to the Court House and take Hod and Dennis out. It was received with applause, and to the Court House the festive company adjourned. Of course the crowd gathered as they marched, and in ten minutes two thousand men were besieging the building, and a dozen self-constituted leaders were banging at the principal door. To their disgust they found that Hod and Dennis had been liberated an hour before. The sheriff had had the wit to bring them before a magistrate for contempt in a quiet afternoon session. The magistrate had given them the alternative of fifty dollars' fine or of two months imprisonment. Hod, who was a man of means, had paid the fine for both. But on a hint from one of the sheriff's officers that they might be "wanted" on a much graver offence the next day, they had sped to the evening express, and were now well out of his jurisdiction. The army of liberation found their work done to their hand.

"Let's serenade old Trustum, hang him! Let's teach Jack Wolff a little Rocky Mountain law!" This was the cry of one of the disappointed leaders. And the hundred or two who heard cheered, and the whole uncertain mass of men who did not hear surged slowly down through Lewis Avenue to the unconscious homes of the unpopular judges.

John Wolff was lying on the sofa. Rachel was playing to him a song without words. The front door opened, and Ephraim Tait dashed in.

"Take the Doctor and the baby and Suse. Don't stop for nothin'. Cut through the garden to the little orchard, drop 'em over the wall, and then pack 'em to my house. Jedge, you go fust. It's you they's after. I'll pack the babies with Miss Wolff."

Nor did Ephraim tolerate any delay for counsel. When babies and Jedge and "Miss Wolff" were safely in the orchard he returned to the house. He put out the gas in the sitting-room, lighted it in the study, put on Judge Wolff's dressing-jacket and cap which he found there, and opened a volume of Reports to read.

In two minutes after, a peal at the door-bell sounded. In a moment more a brickbat through the office window struck the pipe of the chandelier. The metal gave way, and a stream of fire poured down from the ceiling on the table below. A storm of brickbats and other missiles followed. Ephraim took refuge in the dark sitting-room, and did not venture out to extinguish the papers which were blazing on the table. One crash, as a heavy blow broke the window sash, was followed by an inroad from the piazza of a dozen men.

"Here is the sneakin' cuss. Off with him. Who's got handcuffs now?" And a bit of cord brought for the purpose was thrown round Ephraim's neck rather as a type of subjection, and he was hustled by a dozen men into the dark hall and street. Strange to say, in an agony of apparent terror, he pressed his handkerchief to his face, and seemed almost willing to leave the blaze behind him.

An express wagon was at the door. "In with him! in with him! Take him to Gus Mitchell's. We'll try him. We'll teach him the law of the Rockies! Hump yourself, 'squire!" This was the cry of the leader of the whole foray.

And the captive silently mounted the cart, still sobbing in his handkerchief. Hatless, and with no sign of resolution, he permitted himself to be held by the two brutes who took the seat with him.

It was not till the wagon arrived at Mitchell's, well in advance of its escort, that Ephraim threw all disguise away.

"I'll teach yer Rocky Mountain law!" he cried, as he gave one of the two a blow which pitched him from the wagon. "I'll interpret the statutes for yer, Jem Blowers!" he said to the other, as he twisted his neck cloth by a rapid hold behind his neck, and wrenched the poor wretch from his place. "Ef yer want to fight, any of you, yer know were there's fightin' to be done." But the horses, frightened, were backing the wagon wildly, and when Ephraim jumped off he disappeared in the darkness.

Ephraim Tait was a bachelor. Or if there were any

Mrs. Taits in one or another region in which he had travelled, they were never alluded to by him or his intimate friends. But Rachel and her husband and the children found the latch-string out, and when at last they dared strike a light, a house of two rooms, thoroughly neat and comfortable. In these rooms the three children were completely at home. They had often spent long afternoons there with Ephraim, in admiration, too strong for words, of the devices of his housekeeping.

Meanwhile the sheriff had not been asleep. He had not troubled himself much by reliance on the police of the infant city, so called. He had sent to the Military Academy, and at the moment when the mob left Mitchell's he had spoken through the telephone to the professor. The young men liked no better errand. They had two miles at double-quick in which to blow off their steam. They met a deputy sheriff just before they came to the city pavement. And so it happened, that in less than sixty seconds from the moment when the express wagon left Judge Wolff's house, the flinging of brickbats ceased suddenly as a blaze of bayonets appeared when the column wheeled into the avenue. The sheriff on horseback rode in advance and cried, " Clear this street, and clear it quick !" with one or two unnecessary adjurations.

The street was deserted in an instant by all but the improvised soldiers. They had their hands full in extinguishing the fire.

The riot was over. The sheriff arrested ten of the most guilty men in their drunken sleep at six the next morning. The *Evening Blackguard* published a flaming leader, pointing the finger of scorn on all who had instigated it, or seduced these misguided men. Order reigned in Warsaw.

But when poor Rachel and her children went back to their pretty home, there were not five panes of glass unbroken. The keyboard of the piano had been crushed by a paving stone hurled by some Ajax. Every one of John Wolff's historical picture frames was demolished. Indeed, it was almost by miracle that the fire had been put out, after it gained the way it had made in the office.

Rachel took her poor homeless birds to the Governor's open house. And she never lived in that wrecked home again.

CHAPTER XIX.

BACK AGAIN.

"Through Eden took their solitary way."
Paradise Lost.

No! It was certain that in such an aspect of affairs no party would nominate John Wolff for judge at the next election. If he opened his office at his house, it was simply to expose his family to insult and perhaps to danger—to run all the gauntlet of boycotting, and for nothing. John declined a flattering proposal from Mr. Talfourd that he should remove to New York, and so soon as he could free his old home at the Shaft from his tenants he took his wife and children there to begin life again.

And Rachel's kitchen was established in the log-cabin which to the original Huddleston, weary of camp life, seemed a palace. She would not let her husband depreciate her surroundings. "How much better off we are than we were, even with your ulster for both in the fog! How much better off I am than when Miss Goddard was abusing me because my accounts did not please her! How could I be unhappy when the children are so well?"

As for the children, it need not be said that they greatly preferred the delights of the Shaft to the luxuries of the metropolis. There had been talk of a school in town. Little danger was there now of such imprisonment in Huddleston. Ephraim Tait had conducted the removal of the household goods. He was so well pleased with the outlook at the Shaft that he removed his household goods there also. And the "doctor" and Susie had his invaluable assistance in their education in arts of the trapper and the angler. Indeed the "doctor" was heard to confide to Susie that Ephraim was teaching him how to "prospect," and that he knew he should create a shaft of his own some day, and that his father would be rich again, and Huddleston's a great city. From that time, when the children took their lunch with them into the thicket, it was with private expectations that before night the great discovery would be made, and before morning mamma would have her new piano.

And Rachel? She declared that life passed more smoothly than it had for any time in five years. In the first place, her husband was at home most of the time. When the court met at Blood's he was there, and sometimes in another county. But he was not away now three quarters of his life. As for her own time, she was responsible for breakfast, dinner, and supper, with the help of her little Susie. But when these three things were done and the kitchen and pantry were in order, Rachel had more time to herself than she had had with her round of social cares and duties, as the president of countless charities and 'a general leader of society. Washing day of course was a nuisance. That was foreordained when Eve left Paradise with Adam. And although Adam still loved Eve, even he could not wholly relieve her in that business of cleaning the skins when they were dirty. But John could and did provide the best machinery there was. He would send over from Blood's the last sweet thing in wringers, and would expect her to destroy linen and buttons with alkalies.

Ephraim Tait brought her in a conduit, from the edge of an infant glacier, the purest and "softest" of water. And Rachel herself glorified the laundry business with all the glamour which Nausicaa threw about it.

She took a good deal of comfort from Madame Levi and Sal Kootz and others of the women of the Shaft, who had held by its fortunes when more prosperous persons had abandoned it. The range of life which these women had lived in when with young husbands, who had the miner's gadfly, which drove them from home to home, was marvellous. And after such first husbands died, by one violent death or another, the number of after husbands who had claimed them in turn, in the paucity of women in the earlier camps, would have staggered even Miss Braddon or the Chief of the Sadducees. As life declined and husbands ceased, these women took up a motherly care, perhaps of a camp of twenty of the "boys," as they loved to call these grizzled men. Their power in the community within certain points was very large, and Rachel found that there were few subjects at all within their range, where she could not learn much from their rare and racy experience. For the law of selection had applied. If they had not been very remarkable women they could not have lived through all that they had endured.

But the Shaft had woefully declined in all the signs and realities of prosperity, since those golden days when we saw it before, when it even dictated the names of candidates to State conventions. The particular Carbonate which Huddleston had struck, which had built up a lively little town about his shaft, had given out somewhat inexplicably. Even skilful miners could not understand what account to give of so sudden a failure. Other shafts, which had been started as near as mining law permits to Huddleston's, had never been as successful as their owners had pretended. Companies had been organized in Chicago and at the East, on the strength of favorable reports on these shafts and the well-known wealth which came out from Huddleston's. And these companies had spent a great deal of money in "developing their property." They had developed it in that original sense that they had opened it out to the influences of the sun, rain, and air, but in that developed condition the property remained. The stockholders received no returns; they even became tired of paying dividends. They recalled their engineers and workmen, and so the population of Huddleston's declined. " A few of us stick by," said John Wolff, as he was talking with some friends at Blood's. " Some, as I do, because we have some interests there, which some one must take care of, and we have nothing to pay an agent for letting them alone. Some stay because they have no money to move away with. And two or three enthusiasts stay because they have boundless faith in the future of the Shaft. They have told the Eastern world so long that here was the great centre of the mining interest of mankind that they believe it themselves, and forget that this may be like the centre of the solar system, where some people say there is nothing. Then, as in all mining camps, we have one or two hermits. That Englishman whom the boys call the Duke lives six or eight miles above us. He walks over sometimes for candles and hard-tack and powder and salt, and he is apt to look in and make my wife play Schumann to him. And I'll tell you who we have, Frank—your classmate Trecothick lives three or four miles over the divide. My boys stumbled in on his cabin one day, and he treated them to chocolate. He told me he was translating the fragments of Musæus;

that they had never been properly edited. And I told him that I thought that was very probable."

"Queer fellow," replied Frank Edes; "he always was. I hope the wildcats like his translations. I must come over and see him. He may like to help me about my Hesiod." And they all laughed at the outspurt of the classics beneath the shades of this strange Olympus.

Yes! there was society of a kind—wild and tame, grand and simple—if one were willing to take it or knew where to look for it. But even with all these seductions, life at Huddleston's Shaft was more simple than life at the capital. It reminded Rachel of the old Hitchin days. And sometimes she and John had a tramp through brooks, and over rocks and stumps which seemed like very happy days in Waterville—days no happier than these. Days like Waterville, one says, only, where then were these stout boys and this little girl who run before so adventurously, or who follow behind laden so heavily with woodland treasures?

And in the second summer of their stay here, Rachel's second little girl came to her. And in all that season of care and anxious waiting and grateful rest, the quaint, queer old women of the camp hovered round her, with a set of tender forest courtesies which made her think of the good fairies in the German Fairy tales. And when the little darling opened her eyes upon the light, she was surrounded with ministrations such as no science of Paris or Vienna could command or could improve upon. "I declare to you," said Rachel, in writing afterward to Cecilia, "if my courage had been equal to my gratitude I should have called the baby Sal, or Scindy, or Bets, or Poll, in utter thankfulness to these dear old crones, who are, indeed, more than godmothers to her. And if they will endue her with their unselfish, wise, queer, jolly, happy, kindly, nature-loving ways, why, I shall always thank God that my darling is born to me in what people call a wilderness."

And the little Susan had become a girl of nine years old. She had asked her father for a hatchet because she wanted to build herself a wigwam, and, to Rachel's horror, he had given it to her. She considered herself quite competent to attend to the baby while her mother was ironing or when she went across the creek to take care of Old Bets, when Old Bets had that bad fall in the run. And she was.

One morning Rachel fitted out all the three elders for a day's expedition. The boys carried the provant, Susie had the towels and other "outfit" for bathing, and, by agreement, they met Ephraim punctually at the mill. Then by a trail well known to him, he led them two or three miles to what the children called his "secret." It proved to be a place where by chopping down a dozen trees he had repaired an old beaver's dam so that he had set back the water over a piece of pretty greensward.

"Jest the place for you to larn to swim in," said the delighted old man, "and now I'm the man wot's goin' to larn ye."

The joy of old days in Marblehead Harbor sparkled in his eyes. And to Susie all the memories of the old Baikal days, of which she had made her mother tell her, came up, and the bliss of heaven was before her. It was for this that mamma had packed up the bathing things!

Many other joys illuminated that day. Twenty times did the erring arrow from Will's bow miss twenty rabbits, so called for want of a better name. But twice, what the poets would call his unerring shaft, spitted the little beasts, and so he had a triumphant trophy of victory to carry home. After a day of the wildest life, such as made Susie feel herself in every regard the equal of Mirandy, the Ute girl whom she dimly remembered in her mother's kitchen, they were unwillingly girding up their loins to return home, when a cry from above, almost of distress, startled them.

"You stay ware yer be," said Ephraim.. "Don't move, one on yer, tell I come back. Won't be gone long."

Nor was he. He found in the wooded intervale above, a messenger from Tucker's Cross Roads who had lost his way. Misled by an old corduroy road long since disused, which had been laid in the palmy days of the Atlas Company's lavishness, the poor fellow—"Nothin' but a tender-foot!" said Ephraim, as he apologized for him—had crossed into the thickest growth of the new wood. This always grows closest where the sunlight has once been let in. The tender-foot was pushing his horse as well as he knew how, when the poor creature's leg slipped through a hole between two logs, and he fell, in agony. That was clear enough. Whether the leg were broken remained to be seen.

"Stay jest ware ye be," said Ephraim, when he had diagnosed the position. "Stay ware ye be. Sit on his head, jes' so. Don't ye move tell I come back." And the tender-foot obeyed.

Ephraim went for his charges, thinking the delay would frighten them. Then, with the crow which he had at the dam for his log-rolling, and his inseparable axe, he appeared at the scene of disaster. Few angels from heaven without such tools would have seemed to the tender-foot to be visitors as acceptable. Some skilful chopping, a good deal of prying, with even little Bill rolling in stones and bits of wood under the logs as they rose, ended in the happy starting up of the imprisoned beast. His leg was bleeding, but the bone was not broken. Susie ran and brought her towels, and the gash was skilfully sewed and bandaged.

"Now, wot blamed nonsense sent ye here?" said Ephraim, after the tender-foot was open to inquiry. "Don't ye know that the Atlas is all blown higher nor a kite these six years?"

"I don't know nothin' about the Atlas," said the boy, tired and discouraged. "They sent me with a message to the Shaft, 'n they said I should find the way."

"'N ye didn't," said Ephraim, sententiously. "Lucky for you we wus here. Now you come along on foot, ef your feet ain't tender; ef they be, stay here till to-morrow mornin'," he added, in a grim jest by the way of rebuking the boy that he had lived for so few months in the mountains.

But with all Ephraim's assumed superiority, his native honor held him back from asking why a message to the Shaft were so important, or to whom the boy came. The old days of a Star Route mail to the Shaft had long gone by. It depended now for its news on a weekly mail from Tucker's.

It was not till they came within sight of the light which Rachel had set in the window for them—a little anxious, to tell the truth, now that the sun had gone down so long—that Ephraim said, not austerely:

"Ware be ye goin'? Do you know the Shaft, now you've come?"

No, the poor tender-foot did not know. It was a telegraphic despatch he had.

"For the Jedge, most likely," said Ephraim. "Only generally he leaves 'em word ware he is. Mebbe he forgot. You come in, and we'll see."

And Rachel at the door welcomed the victors. Duly she admired the "rabbits," and promised that papa should have them in a pie when he appeared. And she would not tell him who killed them till the right moment came. And Ephraim praised the children volubly.

"Never woz children thet woz so little tendsome," said he, with pride. And he was sure Susie would soon swim as well as her mother.

Then all parties turned to the tender-foot.

He produced his despatch—one of those well known yellow envelopes of which in old days of the circuit Rachel had opened so many.

Edmund Randolph to John Wolff.

"ATTORNEY-GENERAL'S OFFICE,
"WASHINGTON, August 29, 1895.

"We are very desirous to retain your services as assistant counsel with Messrs. Talfourd and Dexter to see to the rights of the government in the closed mail and transportation cases. The other counsel meet me on the sixth proximo here. Can you be here then? Answer. Draw on me, if you wish, by telegraph for any expenses or retainer in advance.

"EDMUND RANDOLPH, D. H."

The reader will observe that this was in the second administration of John Fisher.

CHAPTER XX.

RACHEL'S ANSWER.

"Resolve my doubt."
Henry VI.

To this despatch, written by a pencil almost vermilion, as she saw, Rachel had to answer. Not at the moment. For nothing was more clear than that the tender-foot could not go back to Tucker's in the darkness. But with the first gray of morning he must be started on his way. She gave him his supper and put him to bed. Ephraim promised to provide another horse for him should his own prove incapable, as seemed probable.

"Ef his own feet wasn't tender," said Ephraim, with a grim smile to little Bill, "he could go on them. But they be."

Then Rachel heard once more, with full sympathy and praise, the experiences of the day. The wonderful successes in the chase, the two baths, how Susie kept up for three strokes, and how brave Bill was in the water, were all repeated in detail. She put her little birds to bed and came down to her despatch.

How long her husband's present absence would be she hardly knew. Her communications with Ethelred, the county town where he was trying a difficult mining case, were much more intricate than those with Edwards's or Tucker's. "Do not be frightened," he had said, "till you hear me say I am dead." She could not get a letter to him at Ethelred for two days. Again, she did not know if he could be at Washington at the time named. And, thirdly, she did not know if he would want to go.

Yet she must answer the vermilion edict.

She sat, without writing, turning over the ifs and buts in her mind as she darned an enormous hole in Will's stocking. She knew she could justify herself to her husband for an answer accepting the proposal. A hundred times she had heard him say that, in a lazy world, action is generally more needed than rest, that Belial, the devil of laziness, always suggests that nothing should be done, and that angels of light therefore prefer to do a thing than not to do it, other things being equal.

All this was favorite gospel with John Wolff.

But against this the suggestion was obvious that, whether this were a lazy world or not, John Wolff was not lazy. He was hard at work. He was hard at work now. Would he thank Rachel for mixing him up again on the same side with those Talfourd people? He had certainly declined to have anything to do with Mr. Talfourd before.

And Rachel took another stocking, with a hole still larger in the heel.

As she adjusted in it a smooth quartz pebble which Bill had brought her from the Cañon, a voice clear and distinct from Aunt Lois's wisdom, in the dear old Hitchin days, spoke out again in her memory:

"If you are in doubt, take the trick." So half an hour before what Ephraim called "sun-up" the messenger was started with his answer.

"And so," said Rachel to her husband, when he came home unexpectedly the evening after, "I wrote the despatch, and here is a copy of it:

"'Mr. John Wolff will be in Washington at the meeting proposed, if possible.

"'RACHEL WOLFF.'

"Now, if you do not want to go you can say it proves impossible, and you can always shelter yourself under your wife's imbecility. That is an advantage married men have," said Rachel. "And, to confess the truth, married women have a similar advantage."

"In this case," said John, "there is no doubt that my old rule holds."

"I am so glad you say so," said she.

"What is papa's old rule?" asked that wise little Susie.

"This is the rule, Poll," said her father, gravely. "When you have a choice to make, whether to do a thing you have never done, or to sit still, and there is nothing wrong in the thing itself, it is generally best to do it.

"When you are older, you shall read Bettina's letters; that is where I found it."

"I remember you said so," said the child's mother. "I have looked for it there, and I found no such thing."

"Was it perhaps in 'Fanny Kemble's Diary'?"

So John Wolff went to Washington.

John Wolff to Rachel Wolff.

"999 I STREET, N. W.,
"WASHINGTON, September 6, 1895.

"MY DEAR CHILD: We have had a day as is a day. I turned up at Riggs's at seven and ordered a bath. After half an hour's scouring, most of the dust and alkali were floating down to the Potomac or elsewhere, and I felt alive again. I found a note from Randolph, and met them all at nine, which is early here. They have let things drift to a point inconceivable. But they have had the worst advice. It all comes out why that wretch Cotterell blew his brains out. He had held the government retainer, and had sold himself to the —— devil. I had better not mention names else. My dear, I never was quite so near all infamy as I was when we overhauled this evidence. Talfourd, who is a prince among men, as I suspected before, had been aghast. He had told Randolph, who is perfectly clean, though slow as a mule, that he would not go on with them one inch unless they had some man who understood what he called mountain practice. He said, of course, he must be a decent man, and was pleased to name me.

"Whether we shall pull through, or whether Cotterell's senior and chief, whom I named inadvertently above, will be too much for us, a good God knows. But we shall see what we shall see, and do what we can do.

"Before I came away to-day, as I was studying affidavits, Talfourd withdrew with the Attorney-General, and after they had conferred they offered me a retainer. I have accepted it. I am to be the resident counsel here, and take the working oar in this thing here, till we put it through. I am to have offices in the Department of Justice and all the assistance I want. Uncle Sam would grow gray if he knew what that means.

"You will see, of course, that you must get ready to move as soon as I can come for you. I am afraid we must leave most of the things at the Shaft. You will like to keep the piano, and you must consult the experts about your packing. I shall know in a few days when I can come, and I only say this that you need not be wondering. . . ."

And the letter went on into other matters, which need not here be cited. This is enough to indicate what happened. Another new life for Rachel. But this time not alone on one friendly ulster, but with these children; —care, if you please, but comfort unspeakable. She is not seeking her place in the world. Where she and they are together home is ready made.

And John made his flying last visit to Huddleston's Shaft and turned over to one or two young attorneys in the county such matters as he had in hand, which they received not ungratefully, to see to in his absence. For the great Hegira itself, or march across the desert, John could not wait. Nor was it of much importance that he should. For Ephraim Tait had early announced that he should go with the emigrant party. "Hain't bin there since '65, wen we marched up the Avenoo, company front. Last time ah see Old Abe, 'n the last time he see me." With Ephraim at the fore, there was little danger of accident at railroad changes, though there was great certainty of comment and incident.

"Don't go so fast as 'n ole cayoose. Get there quicker ef we went afoot, but savvy, yer mother would get tired." Such was his comment to the eager Will as they crossed the plains at the rate of fifty miles an hour.

And the readers of these little sketches of Rachel's life must take their leave of her in Washington. For there, as it proved, was to be the longest anchorage for this storm-tossed girl, who said of herself that her life was typified when she sank ten feet under water in the Atlantic, and then rose again as quickly to light and air. Ah me, Rachel! is that any peculiarity of your life? Is there one of us who might not say the same thing?

Yes. It proved, as had been suspected, that this business of the closed mail and transportation cases was not to be settled in three months or in six. Indeed, this was but the bugle call for that great contest which in years upon years, before the people and the courts, was to decide forever, as sanguine men hoped, whether two or three gigantic corporations were to control and supervise the Government of the United States, or whether the People of the United States should supervise and control them. In Randolph, Talfourd, and Wolff, back to back after the fashion of the bayonet manual of France, the country had three paladins at last who understood each other, who believed in the country, and who, in years upon years of every simoom of dust and every tempest of rage, never lost hope for one minute, never announced one victory before it was won, never closed one eye upon any device of intrigue, and in the end they were those who established the Supremacy of the People. Randolph could not stand the strain. It was in the administration of the younger Clinton that this thing came to a close. And the day after the great decision Randolph was found dead in his bed with the smile of peace and triumph upon his lips. Success had lifted him from service here to service higher.

Talfourd and Wolff followed him to the grave. And as it closed upon him, Talfourd bade Wolff good-by.

"Yes, I shall go round the world, I believe. There may be places in Siam and Japan where people will not talk to me of this thing which has finished poor Randolph. I take my wife with me, and shall not see you for three years."

And, when John Wolff returned to his home, he found a note from the President asking if he might name him for the vacant seat on the Supreme Bench.

Perhaps such condensed statements of history are too grave for the younger readers of this tale, or perhaps they think so. If they live till the end of this century they will thank Rachel and John Wolff for turning their thoughts that way, even when reading for relaxation. For such readers, however, fuller account shall be given of one or two details of Rachel's life.

No. She had no time for the washtub or for the ironing-table now. The Judge sometimes said that it would be better for him if she had—that his linen would be more irreproachable, and the tenure of his buttons more permanent. Little time had she for Schumann and Wagner. But she would not exile them wholly. And when her gay reception parties of Tuesday afternoons melted away, there were generally two or three of the elect of the elect who loitered; and after they had settled who that queer woman was who had poppies in her corsage, and that strange man with the cross, who spoke such atrocious German, as the twilight hemmed them in, Rachel would be persuaded to turn her back to the comforted and comfortable group, and play something, just as she had been persuaded on the evening when Ephraim Tait offered them his hospitality so suddenly.

But one episode must be told separately, or the story will be too incomplete, even for a hurried reader.

CHAPTER XXI.

NEW YEAR'S DAY INDEED.

> " Another year,
> Alas! how swiftly do these years fleet by."
> *Love and Politics.*

THAT is a very queer feeling which comes over people when the name of the century changes. Even to change 1884 to 1885 is a jerk—a jerk in which sometimes the thread of memory breaks, and the old machine does not run precisely. But to change 1899 into 1900, this seems to rock the very foundations of the world.

When that hoary, wicked, torturing, analyzing, and bloody, worthless old eighteenth century gave signal of going out—when 1799 gave way to 1800—all America was touched to the heart, as day after day, to city or to hamlet, crept along the news that George Washington was dead. In nearly three-score and ten years he had given to the hoary old calendar its brightest name. What would this new-born eighteen hundred have to offer of glory or of shame?

Vain to say that 1800 is only the end of the old century, and that we must wait another year before a new century begins!

A great deal is in a name, dear Juliet, and when the year is once called 1800, people will look eastward and welcome the rising sun.

But this is all that these pages shall reveal of the outward surroundings, the hopes or the fears, with which, by previous appointment made, Judge Wolff and his wife, and Thomas Poore and his, met at the Delmonico's of the day for lunch, before going to Tiffany's as by the old appointment. They were to give the history of the shares in the Stocking-Loom, and they were to determine what should be the investment of the proceeds.

But where was Miss Ruth Cordis? Had she forgotten the appointment? Had she crossed the seas or the continent? Or had consumption like a worm in the bud preyed on her fair cheek and consigned her to an early grave?

Dear reader, you may spare your tears. You do not recognize the girl of sixteen whom you last saw when Satan entered into her and she rebuffed Miss Willard, when she also had been possessed by him or one of his.

Too many years have passed, and the "Fortunes of Ruth" have been too much varied for her to escape the changes which will come. But, let us confess it, this is Ruth Cordis who comes in with Tom Poore; who takes Rachel by both hands and kisses her so exuberantly. Yes, Ruth Cordis and Mrs. Thomas Poore are one and the same!

This book is not the "Fortunes of Ruth." This book must not attempt to tell her history. But this may be told briefly, that when Thomas Poore had bravely taken down his porcelain picture and sent it anonymously to Miss Finley, he did his best as well to eradicate her image from his heart. In that duty, what more natural than that, when he heard one day that Miss Ruth Cordis was at Mrs. Allibone's on a visit, he should call on her to see her and to talk over old times? They talked over old times and new times. They talked about Rachel, about Aunt Lois Winchell, about Hitchin, about everything except the New England Stocking Company. They talked about books and music and the opera and the play. They talked about Ruth's plans for Europe, and the route her father was going to take there. It happened—who knows how?—that Mr. Poore met them in this summer "outing." They met at Brussels, and they went together to Cologne and up the Rhine. As it happened, his route and theirs were very much the same. And the end of the journey was that when they had come home they had agreed to take a longer journey together. And this is how and why it happened that they two came together to Delmonico's, if it were Delmonico's, as has been told.

As for John Wolff, he came because Rachel would not come without him.

"I have brought here my copy of the 'Arabian Nights,'" said Tom Poore, after his introduction to Judge Wolff was happily over, "and here is a picture of us all. See, here are the 'Tales of the Three Calendars.' I never knew before what a calendar was. The only other place where he appears in literature is in John Gilpin. But we are three Calendars. It appears that Calendars are shareholders in a Stocking-Loom Company.

"Now listen to the

"*Tale of the First Calendar.*

"When I left the party at Mrs. Barnard's I carried my certificate of stock with me, and I put it under my pillow when I went to bed."

"Nonsense," said his wife; "you did no such thing, and you know it."

"Second Calendar," replied Tom Poore, "you may

tell your story when your turn comes. Let me tell mine now.

"Under my pillow the shares reposed. In the night my good genie spoke to me:

"'Tom,' said the genie, 'keep what you've got, and get what you can.'

"I obeyed. I bought me three hundred other shares in the company. The other stockholders were surprised, and made me treasurer. I did not go to Bussora. I stayed at home. I traded with the shares, and I sold the stockings. Before I knew it the shares were worth $500 each, and I was a rich man. The original certificate I sold when the market was at the highest. The panic came, and all the stocks went down like mad, and with the proceeds of that sale I bought three shares. The panic ended, and the shares rose again steadily for five years, when I sold again. The crash of 1893 came, and everybody supposed manufacturing was at an end. At the lowest depression I bought Stocking shares again. And so on, and so on. My original share, which cost two dollars and a half, has been in turn six hundred and seventy dollars, then three shares, then seventeen hundred and thirty-one dollars, then eleven shares. When the company sold out and wound up two years ago, the eleven shares yielded six thousand and fifty dollars, and here it is for the disposition of the conspirators."

Tom Poore beckoned to a quiet man who was standing at the side of the room, and he brought a little travelling-bag. Tom opened it and lifted out a gold sugar loaf weighing more than twenty pounds, which he set in the middle of the table.

"This," said he, "is the end of the First Calendar's story."

Story of the Second Calendar.

"I am sorry to say," said Mrs. Poore, "what my husband does not appear to know, that in the improved versions of the 'Arabian Nights' the 'Calendars' appear as 'Royal Mendicants.' If Mrs. Wolff and I appear in that character before this distinguished and learned Judge, I hope he will remember that it is my husband who has assumed it, and not either of us ladies. We did not receive the shares as mendicants. It was a mendicant, perhaps, who thrust them upon us, as Miss Willard said.

"On the sad fate of Miss Willard, I will say nothing.

"For myself, not many years after THE SHARE fell into my possession, I intrusted all my worldly goods and the keeping of them to the young man who has just now addressed you. He consented to add, from year to year, the interest of his share, of which but for two years he has said nothing, to the interest of mine. I preferred to direct the use of this interest, although until my marriage I had let it accumulate.

"Visiting dear Hannah Valentine one summer, who is now Mrs. Elkanah Hornby, I found her husband evidently failing in strength, and that the oversight of her four lovely children came mostly upon her. The next year I found, and I was not surprised to find, that he had died in the spring.

"Talking with Hannah, I found that she hated to give up the dear old home. She hated to leave Hitchin. John Hornby, in a way, carried on the farm. But you know what a Hitchin farm is. Elkanah had left her a little 'in the bank,' as they say. Hannah was prudence and wisdom itself as a manager. 'But there is very little ready money, Ruth,' she said, with that lovely smile of hers.

"No inspiration came to me then. But in September, when the mother of one of my Sunday-school children died and left her an orphan, I wrote to Hannah, and I asked her if she would take Gertrude Tusan to live with her, and would bring her up in the good old Hitchin ways, if I would pay her one hundred and fifty dollars a year. Hannah answered as if I had been an angel from heaven, offering her a lily, a harp, and a crown. Gertrude went. One half the Stocking dividend for that year paid for her. It was 'ready money' to Hannah, and Gertrude had the most blessed home. The next year Tom Tusan, Gertrude's brother, went to make her a visit. But he never came back. And I sent a hundred and fifty dollars more every year for him. The next year we sent down the prettiest little Italian orphan you ever say, and that year my husband made one of these changes in investment he tells you of. Gertrude Tusan was long since Mrs. Rudolph Alston. Mary Tusan, that's a younger sister yet, is Mrs. Walter Wadsworth; but other orphans have been raised up from time to time. The stocks, as you know, have long since been paid off, but the money is in 'Interminable seven per cents,' which, thanks to our friend Judge Wolff, are miles above par in the market. My interest is about three hundred a year. That royal mendicant's,'' and she nodded to her husband, "is three hundred more.

"These six hundred make for four children a perfect home at dear Hannah Valentine's.

"If you care, here are the pictures of the Tusan girls, the Tusan boy, of the Amoretti child; those three are Tucker children; that pretty blonde is a little Swedish girl named Hartstein—there are, I think, nine in all who have been there or are there now. And here is dear Hannah. Have you ever seen a Madonna like her, Judge Wolff?

"This is the end of the second beggar's story."

"And now for Mrs. Wolff," said Mr. Poore, well pleased by his lively wife's exhibit.

The Third Calendar's Story.

"Our story," said Rachel, "for it is really mine and my husband's, is shorter and less eventful. Our share also rose to the fabulous price of six hundred and seventy dollars, and we sold. My first investment was in the piano I took to the mountains, and, I will confess it, in chairs and tables, bedsteads, and also a lovely set of china, Mr. Poore"—and here Rachel looked him steadily in the eye, and he was not sorry that she did—"which I bought that I might recollect three times a day Mr. Thomas Poore's kindness to a friendless girl. But these were only loans to some poor people of our acquaintance. And the Judge there chose to repay it all, and I chose to have him. He invested and waited, and I was frightened as those Rocky Mountain dividends—fifteen per cent, twenty per cent, and the like—came in. I had heard Aunt Lois say, 'High interest, poor security.'"

Tom Poore bowed approval of the general sentiment.

"One day," she continued, "dear dreamy Arthur Clarke came in. I never knew whether he were going to read me a sonnet or talk black-letter law to my husband. This time he came to talk Cinnabar. To his assaying office a wild prospector had brought a heavy lump of stone, thinking it held silver. It did hold quicksilver.

"Arthur had a thousand dollars to put into that mine.

"He wanted my husband to put in another thousand."

"And he did ?" almost screamed Thomas Poore.

"He did."

"You say your husband was one of the first in the New Ydria Mine ?"

"The stock was in my name. I was there and am. I then held one twentieth of the property, now it is only one fortieth. Here are the certificates. They belong to the conspirators." And she laid the titles, almost priceless, on the table.

Even Tom Poore, well balanced as he was, flushed as she quietly told the story. This woman, because she called herself trustee of this fund of hundreds of thousands of dollars, had gone into a wilderness and worked her own hands to the bone without touching a copper of it.

"With the other half," she said, "my husband built the building and provided the endowment for the Rocky Mountain Institute for the Orphan Sons of Miners. That is its real name. But he always insisted that they should pay a good deal of attention to drill and tactics. And it was those boys who saved our house the night of the riot, which you remember, Ruth. We propose, if Mr. Poore will give Mr. Gaudens the sittings for a likeness, to have his statue placed in the hall, by way of introducing the century.

"This is the end of my story."

So they fell to their shrimp salad and Charlotte Russe.

And after the lunch they went to Tiffany's, and, as had been determined, they bought a little diamond ring for Miss Willard.

"It shall be marked," said Tom, ' Out of evil educing good.' "

"It shall not," said his wife. "It shall be marked with that about Joseph, ' God did send me.' "

"No," said Ruth, "it shall be marked, 'Love, Faith, and Hope.'"

And it was.

But they all knew that Miss Willard was abjectly poor. Her crossness had poisoned life for her. As all ill-tempered people do, she had brought punishment on herself. Yet to that ill-temper they owed so much! It was agreed that five thousand dollars of the accumulations should be spent in an annuity for her.

And for the rest it was determined that the Orphan Institute should go on, and that Hannah Hornby's house should be kept as full as she wished it kept, even until she died.

CHAPTER XXII. AND LAST.

OLD FRIENDS AND NEW.

"Come, come, leave business to idlers and fools, they have need of them. Wit be my faculty and pleasure my occupation."—*Congreve.*

Of all cities yet discovered in this world, Washington seems to be that where society has organized itself with most skill. Or is it tenderness? Or is it both? No place exists where the tired and way-worn man of brains and work can take his holiday so easily. As soon as the dust and alkali of travel are washed off, if one may quote John Wolff's letter, some of the most charming houses in the world are open to him, if he be good for anything, and he may take his ease till it is his turn to go back to his grinding. In the pleasant, unaffected homes of people of whom he has heard of all his life—some of whom are rich and some of whom are not rich, but all of whom under that same law of selection have won the respect of their fellows—such a traveller finds the largest variety of society; he knows what the world is; indeed, he is himself at his best.

Of such pretty homes Rachel Wolff's was one of the prettiest. So everybody in Washington knew, and whoever else was forgotten on Tuesday afternoon she was not forgotten. And Rachel had, by instinct or by training, the art of finding out people whom nobody else found, who were at the same time the people the best worth knowing.

What magic was it which kept away from her the tricksters and shysters, the pretenders who are so apt to put in their heads wherever hospitality is easy, and how did she manage to annihilate them? No man can tell what this magic was. But somehow, in that house, the two poles of attraction and repulsion were at their best. The nice people came and the bores stayed away.

It was in the middle of a charming afternoon when talk had been at its liveliest. Fifty people had come and gone, any one of whom would have made the fortune of an afternoon tea-party in any other city in the land. As Rachel stood talking with the German Minister, Sir Henry Jackson came to her.

"My dear Mrs. Wolff, I have a great favor to ask of you, and you are always so good-natured."

"That means," said Rachel to the Baron Grimm, "that I gave him a cup of weak tea yesterday at the Chevalier's. Pray go on, Sir Henry; we will see if I can consistently grant your favor."

"I want to present to you a young countryman of mine; indeed, he comes to me with the best of letters, but he is, oh, so shy."

"Are you not used to that yet, at the Legation?" said Rachel, laughing; "you know we all think that you are modesty itself."

"You are too good," he said; "but I see that you consent, and that you will introduce my young friend, who really deserves it of your kindness, to some of your nice people. What he is good for I do not know, but his father is our distinguished Dr. Balfour, the correlation man."

"Not Dr. Balfour who died last year—Dr. Balfour of Appleby?"

"The same."

"My dear Sir Henry, you do not know how happy you make me. Pray bring your young friend to me at once."

And the frightened boy came, not knowing whether he held his hat or not, and holding it as badly as a hat could be held ; not knowing how to say "Yes" or how to say "No," and whether he should speak English or Choctaw, and wishing indeed that he were in the bottom of the sea. And yet in thirty seconds that poor frightened tender-foot was at ease, had forgotten that he was three thousand miles from home, even had forgotten that he had been so wretched a minute before. "My dear Mr. Balfour, your father was one of the dearest friends I had in the world, and you—I wonder whether I saw you when you were a baby ? Tell me all about dear Appleby, and tell me about Bongate and St. Laurence's and the vicar. Who is the vicar now ? Who is at Sir Robert Tufton's old place ? I saw the death of Mr. Playfair." And so she went on, gossipping about old Appleby days. And, to his amazement and eventual ruin in society, young Mr. Balfour found that the finest woman in Washington knew every inch of his native place as well as he did. His ruin dated from the misfortune that, having always supposed himself to be the most important person in the world, he thus leaped to the other delusion that his distant home was the best known place in it. But on this occasion, for once, if never again, he reaped the full advantage of being born in Appleby. Rachel presented him to the sweetest girl in Washington. She did this with such *empressement* that the girl knew or thought that this stiff young Englishman was somebody. They withdrew for a little, and then Rachel gave the young gentlemen, who were her devoted aids, to understand that if this little Englishman did not have the best that Washington could give during all his stay, they should all be flayed alive, themselves hanged and quartered, and their bones exposed to the malediction of the world. Why this particular oaf was to be so honored no one at first understood. But to those who asked the fewest questions, Rachel eventually condescended to say that Appleby was the place where she was born, that she had seen no one who came from it in many, many years, and that even if the oaf had been an old beggarman from the almshouse, he should have dined with the diplomats at the next state dinner at the White House, had he expressed any desire to do so.

But it was not simply to old townsmen that Rachel was good and kind. Was it a habit which had grown upon her, because she had been herself utterly friendless so often ; or was it a divine instinct, the same which had found friends for her in her loneliness? Something there was—call it gift, call it genius, as you choose— which so worked in Rachel that she always found out friendless people and put them at their very best.

She beckoned Lieutenant Watson to her, and he flew across the room. "Lieutenant Watson, I have not thanked you for the miracle you worked last Tuesday. All the same, I knew you worked it, and I was grateful."

The lieutenant bowed and blushed. He knew perfectly well what she meant. He had discovered at Riggs's the most eminent man of music of his day, who happened to be in America with his daughter. The man of music had not known enough to register his name at the hotel, and the hotel people had sent him up to the sixteenth story. Lieutenant Watson had discovered him, much as Huddleston had discovered the nugget which made his shaft famous. The musician had not been in his attic five minutes before the lieutenant had exhumed him, had abused the gentlemanly clerk of the hotel, and had seen that these distinguished people were placed in rooms worthy of the chapelmaster of the Emperor of Germany. And before the chapelmaster and his daughter were an hour older, they were in full dress and were at Rachel's reception, wondering at the promptness of Washington hospitality.

"I know the miracle, my dear Mr. Watson, though I did not thank you for it at the moment, and to-day I am going to reward you."

"I have my reward already," said the young man, well pleased that his success was known.

"That is very fine, but at this court when we reward people we reward them with something tangible. Now you think I am going to give you a diamond-mounted epaulette, or perhaps that I am going to ask the Secretary of War to advance you forty-seven numbers on the promotion list. Such rewards would be carnal. Indeed, mine are of a much more ethereal character. I am going to introduce you to the finest woman in America."

"I need no introduction," said the lieutenant, bowing low.

"Wait until you have tried before you repeat your compliments. She is in this room now, and you young men are so dull that you haven't found her out. But I had found her out before she had been here two minutes. And you, with all your miracle-working, are so stupid that you have let that creature sit for ten minutes in a *tête-à-tête* with old Mrs. Munroe, who is so deaf that she has not heard one word which my Hebe has spoken to her."

The lieutenant turned toward the *tête-à-tête* chair and looked his astonishment.

"Do not pretend to be astonished. I know more than

you do, and you know I do. Come to me a week hence, and if you say I am wrong you shall have the diamond epaulette and the promotion." And so she presented him to that unassuming, quiet Mary Van Nostrand, the level-headed, bright, quaint, fascinating Nantucket girl, who was the rage of Washington for the rest of the season, and of whom, from the beginning, Watson was the humblest servant.

How had Rachel discovered the capabilities and qualities of this quaint girl in the thirteen words which had passed between them as Mrs. Randolph presented her?

Who shall say? Genius or talent, have it as you choose—only these were the wonders which made her home so charming.

"What can you tell us of our new sovereign, Mrs. Wolff?" said Sir Henry Jackson, as he returned to her at the end of an hour. "I do not mean the new President, of course; we all know him, but what is much more important to you and me, how is it about the President's wife? Will she question us about the catechism, or will she ask me what is the pattern of the Queen's gown?"

"Sir Henry, if you talk any treason in this room you shall never enter it again. Nay, I see the Secretary of State has come in, and he shall say in a cablegram to-night that your presence is disagreeable to this government."

"Indeed, indeed, Mrs. Wolff, I have talked no treason. I have breathed none. I only want to know how to prepare myself for the first reception. My duty is to create the most favorable impression that I can, and the truth is that I am in the least bit weak on the very last questions of the catechism. I know all about the condition of life to which I am called, and just at this moment I am very well satisfied with it."

"Very good. Now you are humble and speak as you ought. I will tell you that she is one of my oldest and dearest friends."

"Oh, Mrs. Wolff, do not exaggerate. Such things can be carried too far, even in diplomacy. She is one of your oldest friends, somewhat as Miss Van Nostrand is, who, as I know, Mrs. Randolph has presented to you this afternoon for the first time. Dearest friend, of course she is, because you are so good to everybody."

"Cannot an ambassador believe anything?" said Rachel. "You know perfectly well that I am not in the service, and that I speak truth 'from native impulse, elemental force.' It is as queer to you as it is to me, but the simple truth is that the first time in my life when I ever saw what a girl calls a party—I mean the first time when I had a new frock given me that I might wear it to a party—I met this lady. So I can tell you frankly that, as I was then fourteen and she was sixteen, she is two years older than I. She was then, probably is now. This was at what we call in New England a 'sewing circle.' Whether such things exist at Windsor I am not quite sure. I was the most frightened person in the room, and Miss Ruth Cordis—that was this lady's name before she was married—was almost as badly frightened as I. Misery likes misery, and we sat down together. I suppose she threaded my needle for me; very likely she held my teacup while I folded up my work. That was the beginning, but we lived together in the same village for two or three years after that, and there are few things we have not done together. I have climbed chestnut trees with her. I have forded brooks with her. I have caught trout with her, and fried them and eaten them wholly unknown to the home people. I have gone to singing-school with her; she has sung one part when I sang another at a school exhibition. Nay, I have even received her confidences on occasions of early passion—confidences which I shall still respect, and shall by no means repeat to her excellent husband. Why, indeed, Sir Henry, from this very gentleman, our new President, we both received queer presents in those prehistoric days. I have mine now, and I dare say she has hers."

"Might a diplomat venture to suggest," said Sir Henry, laughing at this description, "that it might have been a great blessing to this country had the new Chief Magistrate pressed his advances in another direction?"

"No, Sir Henry; diplomats must not talk nonsense. That is the first rule of our service, and I fancy it is in yours. When you come to know Mr. Tom Poore better than you seem to do, you will find that he is a man to whom nobody gives much advice; who is apt in his quiet way to look out for other people more than he looks out for himself; he generally succeeds in what he determines to do, and his friends are glad that he has succeeded.

"But we are old friends, Sir Henry, and if you like to come to me next Tuesday I will tell you all about the new sovereign lady and her present plans. For they are coming directly to this house on Friday, and will stay here until the Clintons leave the White House. Whatever is proper for you to communicate to your government, you shall be told next Tuesday after Mrs. Poore and I have talked it over together."

Let us hope that the communication made to the English Minister on the whole advanced the kingdom of righteousness and truth; that Rachel opened everything that was to be opened, and withheld everything that was to be withheld. For information on that point, however, the reader must turn elsewhere. This book is not the history of the diplomacy of the twentieth century.

The inauguration came and went, and all things were prosperous. Almost as a matter of course Rachel was Ruth's principal counsellor in the mysteries of a life that was so new to her, of the etiquettes of the White House and of the city. The two ladies met, as if they were two school-girls again, and had endless talks of what had passed since Hitchin days—talks mostly of the fortunes of their children, sometimes of those children's health, sometimes of their morals. Thomas Poore managed his affairs with admirable good sense and good humor combined. The traits which had brought him to the front— none of the politicians could tell how—served him when he was at the front. A man who always made friends, and acted as if he had no enemies.

Fortunately for this reader and this author, nothing more need be said here of the politics or statesmanship on which Thomas Poore's cabinet was founded. In the twentieth century it was as true as in the first, that the eternities are Faith, Hope, and Love. On these that administration was founded. Enough here to say that the PEOPLE had triumphed, and that Tom Poore with a firm hand represented them, and terrified all their adversaries.

It is not with his affairs that we are concerned.

The day came at last when his wife was to receive "for the first time." Of course she summoned Rachel to be at her side to help her, with Mrs. Pickering and the pretty Miss Rutledge. As they stood together, wondering who might be the Protesilaus, who should first attack their well-defended line Ruth said to Rachel, "It will be one of your wood-cutters from the Rocky Mountains. Rachel said to Ruth, it will be "Deacon Eberle from Hitchin." The usher threw open the door and announced "The Senator from New York, with Mr. and Mrs. Hudson."

For a few minutes no one else came. The Senator talked with the President, who was an intimate personal and political friend. Mrs. Hudson talked with Ruth Cordis, who is to be remembered in history as Mrs. Thomas Poore. And Rachel for those same minutes entertained the railway magnate, her old friend, Mr. Thomas Hudson.

THE END.

www.ingramcontent.com/pod-product-compliance
Lightning Source LLC
Chambersburg PA
CBHW022017220426
43663CB00007B/1114